The

Golden Rule

of Schmoozing

the authentic practice of
treating others well

by **A**ye **J**aye

with Foreword by Penn & Teller

Sourcebooks, Inc.
Naperville, IL

This publication is designed to provide accurate and authoritative information in regard to the subject matter covered. It is sold with the understanding that the publisher is not engaged in rendering legal, accounting, or other professional service. If legal advice or other expert assistance is required, the services of a competent professional person should be sought.

> *From a Declaration of Principles Jointly Adopted by a Committee of the American Bar Association and a Committee of Publishers and Associations*

Published by Sourcebooks
P.O. Box 372, Naperville, Illinois 60566
(630) 961-3900
FAX: (630) 961-2168

Library of Congress Cataloging-in-Publication Data

Jaye, Aye.
    The golden rule of schmoozing : the authentic practice of treating others well/
by Aye Jaye ; foreword by Penn & Teller.
        p. cm.
    ISBN 1-57071-129-1 (pbk.)
    1. Interpersonal communication. 2. Interpersonal relations.
3. Communication—Psychological aspects. I. Title.
    BF637.C45J39 1998
    158'.2 — dc 20
    JAY   96-41717
                                                                        CIP

Printed and bound in the United States of America.

10 9 8 7 6 5 4 3 2

Contents

Contents

Dedicated to my ladies from A to Z...
Annie, my wife and writing partner, and my daughters, Zsajsha & Z'dra.

ACKNOWLEDGMENTS

Read this last; start reading the book!

To my two main men, Ray Kroc and Fred Turner.

Thanks for the heads up Pete Henseler.

Thanks to Dominique Raccah from Sourcebooks for being schmoozer enough to publish me...and her team, Todd Stocke, Deborah Cross, Renee Calomino, Andy Sardina, and Connie Fritsche.

My love to the tan Greek Goddess, Paula, and her English teacher Susan.

Thanks to Karen Kolberg.

Special thanks to the first picnic table schmoozers:

My soulmate, Roy Bergold
John Haas
John (Jones) Roelandts
Mike Greenfield
Hank & Nan Stothard

Bill Berland
Tom Feeney
Turo & Georgia
Eric "the manly man" Clark
Barb & Mel Shikora

Bergie's Brigade: Susan Leick, Steve Nubie, Nicki Kaphusman, Sue Cox, Tommy Vicini, Jack Doepke, Diane Blake, Tom "no taste" Lines, Linda Briggs, Sarah Rosch, Mary Giangrasso, Marie McDonald, Dave Batt, and April Maroney.

LIFE MENTORS:

To Mom & Dad; Ray & Matka
Judge Jennaro, Jimmy Jennaro, & Jennaro
   Clan
Jack & Ruth Wenzel
Izumi's
Cafe V
Don the Barber

Cab's Bistro
John Hawkes
Kathy Henry
David Brown
Chuck Rubner
Larry Lee
Suds

Rocky & Georgia Felger
Mike Elliott
Sol Steren
James Pihos
Giovannis
Cheryl Berman
Colleen Mather
John Davis
Carlos Desuza
The Bleacher Creatures
Anthony Newley
Mary Miller
Paul Schrage
Ed Rensi
David Green
The Rainman and The Starman
Dan & Heidi Staedler
Lance & Valentina Staedler
Kathy Bergold
Bud Frankel
Allen Brown
Mark Levy
Carol Wolfe
The Badger Boys
Debbie Roelandts
Gino Salomone
III Sheeters
Fran & Al Blechman
Frankie Little
Master Showman Frank Currie
Emmy Winner, Stevie Smith
Master Clown, Barry Lubin (Grandma)
Tommy, Tammy & Amelia Parish
Jack Greenberg
Brad Ball
Ferguson
Dick Helland
Lance Burton
Jack Smith
Tony
Dick Monday
Bob Babisch
Dave "Punkie" Wastig
Vic Thomas
All Joey's, T.O.M.'s & RBB&B Red & Blue
Jim Ragona
Clown Hall of Famer Joe Sherman
Betty Farina
Chatchke
Danny & Pat, Frankie & Elaine, Dorothy & Gordy, and my role model, Maxine
Sandy Christopher
Roz Turner
Samara Turner
Comedy Sportz
DA Yooper Guy

Eddie Elison, Russell Dutsell, Pete Assen, Winney, Jimmy Schuster, Kenny Mayer & Paula Marr
Marty Shaye
Paul Binder
Ronnie Kilroy
Larry Source
John Lavin
Roy Terracina
Bruce Olsen
Emmy Winner, Thom Christopher and his European cast of "12 Angry Men"
Jon LaBracke
Tony Winner, Anthony Crivello
The Baron & Baroness Vomberg, my other family
The brave men and women of the Okauchee Fire Dept.
Mary Haas
Nancy Clark
Sue Berland
Sandy Serdynski
Ken Barun
Sandy Silver
Marty Silbernik
Henry Lienau
Rollie & Adam
Joey Balistrieri, my vocabulary coach
Thanks to the guy who gave me my act, Dean of Magicians Worldwide, Jay Marshall
Linder Kravitz
Mike Quinlan
Joe Telcot
Shelby Yastrow
Joe Talcott
Dean Barrett
The Chief
John Renfrow
R.J. Malano
Bob Collins
Bob Barry
Patrick Czalanski
Clifie Diedrich
Jack Lee
Joe Laughlin
Margi Moose
Mike Gousha
Reitman & Mueller
Dave & Carole
Jill Geisler
Neil Janert
Tom Hooper
Jonathan Green
Mary Kay Riordan
Ralph Chicorel
Stan Nicpon

ACKNOWLEDGMENTS

Dick Steinberg
Mary Grace Catalane
Jim Cantalupo
Palo
John Iverson, the Great Gastby
Karen Bellows
Debbie Gibson
Carl's Command: Jeff, Teddy, Bing, Renee,
Doug, Kim, Jason, Brian, Erika, Lori,
Julie & Gabe
The next big magic couples act to headline in
Vegas, Tony & Juleen Laffan
Marshall, Jay and Tommy V. Which one of
you is going to be? Maybe someone start-
ing with a Z, like Zeke?
J.D
Pat Page, Kevin James & Arturo
Ali Bango
Linda
Jimmy Lombardo
Lionel "the Train" Aldridge
Wayne "the Wall" Embry

Laura Heidtman
Christine & Jeff Emmanuel
Lips Labelle
Donny Bauer
Gonzalo
Eduardo Pená
Variety Club International
C.O.A.
W.C.A.
The Broadcaster's Club
Debbie Holton
Chris Morganson
Kenniston
Showmen's League
Marty Zuckerman
Digger
Chief
Tommy Hanneford
Louie Sherman
Frank Macina
Roy & Josie
The Obies

Special thanks to my spiritual advisors...

Terry Meeuwsen
Dr. Raymond Moody, Jr.
Dr. Billy Graham
Reverend Thomas Oscar Parish, Jr.
Monsignor Murphy
Rabbi Berry
Silberg

Richard Gere
Preacher Moss
The Church Lady
Stuart Smalley
The Psychic Hotline
Penn Fraser Jillette
I'M SO CONFUSED!!!

The following are some of the funniest people I've ever had the privilege of working with, and I give them my warmest thanks. Some of these names you already recognize, the others are on the way.

Carol Leifer
Frank Caliendo
Tim Cavanaugh
Mike Mercury
Scott Henry
Tom Kenny
Julia Sweeney
Ward Hall
John Podlesnik
Lord Coret
Bruce Brinker
Tom Parks
Jay Johnson
Dick Chudnow
Greg Janese
Lewis Black
Sean McKenna
Glenn Gerard
Rob Schneider

Brady Street
Kevin Brandt
Fred Klett
Preacher Moss
Chris Barnes
Darrell Hammond
John Mendoza
Will Durst
Lonny Shore
Gilbert Gottfried
Debi & Mike
Tommy Chong
Brian Green
Judy Tenuta
Emo Phillips
Special thanks to Rosie O'Donnell
Lukeski
Mitsy, Sammy & Pauly Shore
Bob Hope

Billy Crystal
Chris Rock
Bill Hicks
Robin Williams, you clever son of a sitcom
Joey Kola
Earl Chaney
Jim Breuer
Bill Maher
Andy Kaufman
Mike Dirkin
Jay Mohr
Dennis Miller
Bob Goldthwaite
Gary Mule'deer
Carrot Top
Drew Carey
Steve Seagren
Pam Stone
Mark Shilobrit
Mike Preston
Dan Whitney
"Larry the Cable Guy"
Rich Schydner
Jeff Foxworthy
Louie Anderson
George Carlin
David Seebach
Penn & Teller
Jeff Brannon
Jay Leno
Mitchell Walters
John Fox
Mick Lazinski
Rich Hall
Jeff Altman
Tim Allen
Diane Ford
Elayne Boosler
Rita Rudner
Richard Belzer
Peter Reveen
Jeff Campbell

Bello Nock
Bob Parkinson
Ron Schultz
Bobby Hunt
Ricky Jay
Doctor Boese
Mark Lundholm
Joe Cortese
Holly Ignatowski
Pat Morita
Angelo Farina
Stevie Vento
Hugh Donaldson
John Weiss
Dobie Maxwell
Tim & Tom
The Comedy Kitchen
Carl Wolfe
Stu, Sonny & Dink
Toby Kidd
David Jinn
Leon "Buttons" McBride
Frosty Little
Peggy Williams
Dr. Snowberg
Milwaukee Clown Hall of Fame Museum and Katherine O'Dell
Cecilee Conkling
David Kiser
Eric Michael Gilette
Jim Ragona
Peter Pitofsky
David Larible
Emmet, Lou, Otto, and Mack
The Milwaukee Circus Parade
Baraboo Circus Museum
Bob Parkinson
To everybody who's gutsy enough to own a comedy club and anybody who's savvy enough to book comics
Last, but not least, "Hail Shecky"

Finally, thanks to everyone who fed me a meal as a kid. Who? If I forgot your name, put it here:

FOREWORD BY
PENN & TELLER

Okay, so you want a little proof of how much Aye Jaye knows about schmoozing? You want that? Okay, if you're in the bookstore, pick up the next book on the shelf (the next book that isn't by Aye Jaye—if you just picked up another copy of the same book, buy both—you need all the help you can get). Do you see a Foreword by Penn & Teller? No, you don't. And do you know why you don't? Because we don't write forewords. Why should we pimp someone else's book when we have our own books to sell?

So that's the power of schmoozing—two, overworked, self-obsessed guys taking the time to write a foreword for some schmoozing comic. Why? Because he's been schmoozing the bejeezus out of us for nineteen years.

Even without the schmooze, we'd still love Aye Jaye. He tells great stories, always says the right thing, he's funny, entertaining, he leaves great jokes on our voice mail, he sends goofy little gifts, he takes us to dinner, he makes the world a better place—hey wait a minute, that's schmoozing.

If Aye Jaye can get us to write a foreword for his book, he can sure as hell teach you what you need to know to get what you want and have a good time doing it.

I just hope you don't all want forewords to your books—we have our own lives to live.

—Penn & Teller

P.S. While you're here at the bookstore, go around the corner and pick up our new book *Penn & Teller's How to Play in Traffic*. Hey, who's that handsome guy on page 175?

INTRODUCTION

From the Author

Welcome to the wide, wide world of schmoozing! You've just picked up this book because you're either a schmoozer already, or you're a "wannabe." Either way, the world is better off because of you. You're the one who probably has an inkling that the world desperately needs schmoozers; you're the one who has enough sense to start the ball rolling toward a saner, less caustic society; and you're the one I want to talk with, because you're curious enough to have opened a book that could very well make a difference in your life and give us global peace. (By the way, if you haven't figured it out by now, I was just schmoozing you.)

So, what is schmoozing? According to *Webster's Unabridged Dictionary*, schmoozing is a Yiddish word that means "to chat" or "to converse idly." In his book, *The Joys of Yiddish*, Leo Rosten defines schmooze as: "Shmooze (shmooz, shmoos, shmues) Hebrew: shmuos (originally) 'things heard'; (in time) 'rumors,' 'idle talk.' Both verb and noun, shmooz means a friendly, gossipy, prolonged, heart-to-heart talk, or friendly, persuasive conversation. 'They had a little shmooz and settled everything.'"

But today there is a common misconception about the meaning of schmooze. For many people, the word has come to suggest a con or trickery, particularly a dishonest technique for "getting as much as you can out of someone without his or her permission or knowledge." It has become synonymous with pulling the wool over a person's eyes. A schmoozer is thought of as a shallow person who makes an ingratiating comment to one's face and says the opposite thing behind one's back. This couldn't be further from the truth! That's not a schmoozer, that's a small-time, no-talent, boot-lickin' scammer.

Don't make the mistake of believing that schmoozing is crass manipulation. It's not. As this book will illustrate, schmoozing is based on age-old principles: Know Thyself; The world is as you see it; As ye sow, so shall ye reap; Do unto others as you would have them do unto you. Unfortunately, we now live in a world where many do unto others and then they move out of town. But it doesn't have to be that way.

Schmoozing is the Golden Rule at full throttle. It's a skill and an art form that encourages people to say, "you've made my day" instead of demanding "make my day." It's a technique for turning others on, not taking others on. A schmoozer is more than a common smooth-talker, he's a "schmooze-talker." A schmoozer is someone who talks to people as if they really mattered—and to her they do.

This country must be schmoozing going into the twenty-first century. Schmoozing is volunteering. In schmoozing, you are volunteering yourself to another person, while at the same time making them feel better about themselves. Through schmoozing, we have a genuine chance to make crime and divorce rates drop, teach kids to respect elders and expect elders to teach kids, make drive-by shootings and highway accident scams a thing of the past, and eliminate the need for disgruntled employees to feel as though a gun is the best way to resolve conflicts.

Schmoozing really does work if it's put into practice on a grand scale. Think about the difference between the way people treat one another in

America versus in a country like Japan, where courtesy has always been the backbone of the culture. (It *has* to be, because in Japan, there are six hundred people per square mile, as opposed to sixty per square mile in America.) During the aftermath of a recent catastrophic earthquake in Japan, there were zero reported instances of looting. People waited patiently in lines for water and food, and even a motorcycle that had been left on the street remained in its place until the rightful owner claimed it a week and a half later.

The subways in Japan are always crowded with commuters. During the winter, when everyone is bundled up in thick coats, there's a man whose job entails pushing and bodyblocking the commuters into the subway cars so the doors can close. Everyone responds to his aggressive behavior with a polite *"domo oragato,"* which means, "Thank you very much." (In the United States, the response to that same action would more than likely be, "Whiplash! You'll be hearing from my lawyer.")

I once lost my wallet in the Shin Juku train station in Tokyo with $2,000 cash, my passport, and my Hyatt hotel key in it. Are you ready for this? Yup, you guessed it—it was returned to the Hyatt!

People say the Japanese are polite, but to my mind, it's just another way of saying that they're expert schmoozers. They know that schmoozing isn't sleazy, it's just smart. It's a win-win situation for everyone.

After all is said and done, all I want to prove is that schmoozers are never losers, and losers are never schmoozers. Listen, schmoozing has taken me around the world five times. (I'm not rich; I was working!) I've met eight Presidents, the Queen of England, Prince Charles, and Prince Andrew. I've worked with glamorous celebrities and the top comics and clowns in the world. I even had my own top-rated kids TV show for six years.

I can't guarantee you'll meet royalty. But as a genuine schmoozer, you might be rewarded with upgraded airline seats, better restaurant service, and a room with a view at hotels. You'll instinctively know the methods you can use with the people you deal with every day...your boss, your spouse, your kids, and the next service person you encounter.

So if you're ready, I'll show you the importance of maintaining a bright outlook no matter what the weather, the way to open the door to a more enjoyable life, and how to make any conversation go both smoothly and "schmoozly." To help you out, I humbly recommend you read this book with a highlighter or pencil nearby so your can mark off the things that you are willing to try and that will work for you.

If you already have a successful schmoozing style, great! When you read this book, you'll see yourself in action, and you might even gain a new idea or two. If you know of anyone who could use a few more of your skills—since a little charm does no harm—then give this book to them with a pat on the back and these words of encouragement, "I know you don't need this, but give it a read and give it to someone you know." And if you're a competent schmoozer, you won't find it back on your desk the next day.

What you are about to read is how I've tried to live my life. I've spent three fourths of my life as a functional illiterate, and schmoozing helped me get through that. As I was making it, I was faking it. But at the end of the day, I was sincere. I truly love people and believe that we're all in this together. I volunteer whenever possible, give what I can afford, and really believe that schmoozers are more givers than takers. I hope this book will make your life easier and friendlier. Fantasize that if it catches on, we can achieve world peace. So, my advice is take a vacation, whatever you think is first-class, once a year, every year. Do the right thing. Brush and floss. And remember, yesterday's history, tomorrow's a mystery, today's a gift—that's why they call it present.

—Aye Jaye

CHAPTER ONE

THE FOUR LAWS OF SCHMOOZING

The First Law of Schmoozing is that there are two kinds of people: schmoozers and losers. Schmoozers are always part of the answer; losers are always part of the problem. Schmoozers generate ideas; losers create excuses. Schmoozers say, "Let me do it for you"; losers say, "That's not my job."

Losers are sheep; Schmoozers are shepherds. Losers say, "It may be possible, but it's too difficult"; schmoozers say, "It may be difficult, but it's not impossible." That's why schmoozers are never losers and losers are never schmoozers.

My ability to schmooze saved my life many times. I've talked my way into jobs and out of being mugged, into marriage and out of speeding tickets. Schmoozing can save you, too. It can save your marriage, your job, and possibly your sanity. It can make your life easier and make you more pleasant.

So how do you actually go about schmoozing? Well, the Second Law of Schmoozing is the practical principle on which everything is based: Leave every situation with people wanting more, not wanting you to go.

Schmoozers are often popular because they're charming, and there's nothing people want more than to be charmed. But that doesn't mean schmoozers are always the center of attention. A good schmoozer helps others feel as though they are the center of attention. In other words, it's important to know when to stop being the life of the party and let the party gather momentum without you.

It's also essential to keep in mind that schmoozing is not just a cocktail party skill. Yes, a good schmoozer shines in a big group event, but as the Third Law of Schmoozing states: You schmooze in twos. In other words, every encounter between two human beings holds the potential for conflict and disagreement, and thus also holds the potential for schmoozing. This includes encounters with spouses, bosses, children, partners, service personnel (cabbies, waiters and waitresses, bus drivers, repairmen, telephone operators), and authorities (cops, City Hall, IRS).

Our modern, fast-paced society makes demands upon our time, our emotions, and our wallets, which makes many of us testy much of the time. Living peacefully on planet earth calls for a reduction of our overactive aggression. Conflict is most often eliminated whenever the tongue connects with the heart—another way of saying "schmoozing."

You might be thinking, "Hold on. Schmoozing with a cabby or a telephone operator? What good would that do? We don't have anything in common. These people don't care about me."

But the point is that everybody cares about themselves, so if you make it clear that you care about them too, you've immediately got at least one thing in common. That's the truth behind the Fourth Law of Schmoozing: People want to be schmoozed. As Mary Poppins so aptly stated, "a spoonful of sugar helps the medicine go down."

If you were a telephone operator, which of the following two scenarios would you want to be party to?

1. "Operator, I'm in a hurry. Give me the number for a person whose name begins with a 'Tz' and ends with a 'ski.' I think his first name is Norquist. NO! I don't know how to spell it. Why do you think I'm asking you? That's why you've got the crummy job. Although maybe you shouldn't, if you're this incompetent."

Or how about a more playful, schmoozful:

2. "Howdy! Before I ask you what I need to ask you, let me tell you who you are: You're that person who used to get straight A's in spelling throughout school. AT&T knew about you when you were in the eighth grade. When you graduated from high school, you were their first draft choice for information operator. Am I right? Of course I am. Now, the name I'm looking for starts with a 'Tz' and ends with a 'ski.' I think his first name is Lumbardo. That's all the information I have, so that's why I'm glad I've got a spelling whiz like you as my operator. Do you think you can help me out? If you can find it, I'll give you the rest of the day off."

If you are like most human beings, the last scenario would be your first choice. It's a healthier and more humane way of connecting with each other. Schmoozing is simply good for the glands. (If cleanliness is next to godliness, then schmoozing is sitting in God's lap.)

I've devised several questions to help you determine whether you are ready to delve more deeply into the art and science of schmoozing. Answer honestly.

- Are you willing to break loose and give 5 percent more than the current tipping rate?

- Are you willing to listen to a joke you've heard before without interrupting to say, "I've heard that one before," or is it possible you can laugh genuinely at his or her presentation?

- Would you choose to be schmoozed instead of directed or bullied into doing something?

- Can you release your suspicious belief that everyone is really trying to get on your good side through positioning and dishonest maneuvers?

- Can you lose preconceived notions of people and try to reach the good nature of others?

If you answered "no" to any of these questions, you could benefit from the ideas in this book. Hell, you *need* this book. They say that you shouldn't enter a kitchen if you fear getting into the stew. In the same vein, don't try schmoozing if you fear success. Later, when your life is collapsing and you suddenly realize why you're ramming a fishing lure in your eye—because it feels better when you stop—then you might be ready to hear how the social salve called schmoozing can aid you with your healing.

CHAPTER TWO

COME BEARING CHATCH

Never Come in Empty-Handed

Two elderly gentlemen had been friends their entire lives. One of them had to move across town, so he called his buddy to give him directions to the new digs. "It's easy," he said. "Get on the Vana Street bus, transfer onto the Sushi bus, get off on Groucho Street. First house on the southeast corner, walk up the stairs and ring the doorbell with your elbow." The second man said, "All right, but why am I ringing the doorbell with my elbow?" And the first man said, "What, you're not carrying anything?"

Try this experiment right now. Pick up an object—a pencil, a paper clip, anything—and if someone is in the room with you, hand them the object. Did they take it? Of course they did, because taking something that is offered is an automatic reflex.

Everyone delights in getting "something for nothing." If you have ever attended a convention, you can see this automatic reflex at work. People walk past booths that are giving away free samples, and at the end of the day, they leave with bulging shopping bags. As the old adage tells us, "People will take a hot stove if it's free."

That's why companies give away millions of free samples daily and why coupons are such a hot advertising item. Just the other day, I saw three jars in the window of the drive-through area of my bank. One jar was filled with small packages of candy, one contained bubble gum, and the other had doggie treats. It looked as if they had all their customers covered!

What the bank is banking on is people's delight in getting a *tchotchke*. *Tchotchke* (pronounced chotch'key) is a Yiddish word meaning a toy or little plaything and can vary in price from a 5 cent gumball to a million-dollar yacht docked in the Caribbean.

Restaurants that offer free matches, toothpicks, or mints after the meal understand the importance of chatch. Successful hotels are successful partly because they offer chatch to win your hearts and pocketbooks: mints on your pillow, free breakfasts, passes to the health club, and activities to keep your children occupied. Every year for Christmas, I receive a lovely fruit basket from my local dry cleaners. Do they get my repeat business? You bet!

Astute businesspeople know it's good business to schmooze you with chatch. And the exact same principle can work for you in your personal life. The Chatch Schmooze is the best icebreaker in the world.

When you were a kid, did you have a favorite aunt, uncle, or friend of the family who you could always count on to bring a little something for you when they visited? My cousin Casey (Casmir) is a perfect example of someone who loves buying chatch. Despite the fact that he was a GI on a limited budget, whenever he came home on leave, he always brought something special for me: a pet rabbit for my magic act, a kit to make lead soldiers, a pistol that shot caps, a motorized Erector Set. He also did stand-up comedy, and when I was a kid with the worst toothache pain in the world, he made me laugh so hard that I totally forgot I had a toothache. The humor was the best chatch I'd ever received. To this day, my cousin Casey has a special prime-time place in my heart.

If you've ever given a gift to someone you care about, you can be sure they probably think of you with the same kind of fondness I have for cousin Casey. But the Chatch Schmooze is just as important—maybe even more so—with strangers. Simply offering someone a piece of gum at the beginning of a conversation is an easy and effective way to give someone chatch. It's fun, no one gets hurt, and everyone comes out a winner. The beauty and fun of this schmooze is that it takes the person receiving the gift by surprise. The natural reflex of a person who has been "gifted" in this manner is to find a way to give something back to you. This reciprocation can take many forms: a smile, more friendly service, a room upgrade, a larger portion of food, or faster seating at a crowded restaurant.

The next time you're at the ski lodge getting ready for a day on the slopes, fill your pockets with half a dozen or so chocolate bars or carry six cups of hot chocolate in a cardboard tray. Now, as you go down the rental line and you come to the first station, lay a cup or a bar on the first kid and ask him if he has any decent skis left. He will disappear into the back, and you'll get a new pair, guaranteed. Next, boots, the same way: ask the attendant if she has anything dry. You're not the only person who's asked for dry boots, but you're probably the only one who's going to get them.

Let me guess what you're thinking, because it's the first question I get when I'm giving schmooze seminars. "Aren't you just trying to get something out of somebody?" Well, yes and no. No, because I go into it expecting nothing more than a smooth and easy encounter; and Yes, because I get joy out of giving and even more joy if something comes out of it and I've really clicked with another human being. Don't be afraid that others might think you are trying to buy their affection. When you give a gift with the intent to delight, the recipient will intuitively know that you're not buying their affection; you're earning it. For all giveaways, I always say, "Whether you can help me or not, this is yours just for trying."

CHATCH FOR SPECIAL OCCASIONS

WEDDINGS

When I receive a wedding invitation, I have the invitation framed in silver, and I present it to the happy couple as a wedding gift. If the bride and groom have a yard, I love to give them an espadrille fruit tree (a one-sided tree that goes against the wall). Great gifts: A house name plaque, a street sign with the family's last name, or a porch swing.

BIRTH OF A BABY

I'll give the parents of a newborn a personalized chocolate candy bar that is made to the exact weight of the baby and has the baby's name, birthdate, and weight printed on the wrapper. Do you want to give a gift that makes a positive impression? You can now buy hand or foot print kits that allow the parents to make a hanging clay memento of their baby's prints. I've also given a gift certificate from a toy store, a share of a kid-oriented blue-chip stock, or a fifty dollar savings bond in the child's name. Fifty dollar bonds cost twenty-five dollars and always leave a positive impression on the parents. At the same time, they teach the kids how to save.

Because I know the importance of Chatch, I'm always on the lookout for possible gift items, and when I find something good, I stock up. I found a perfect-sized suitcase that I keep in my car to store all the chatch I buy on impulse. I call it my Chatch Crash Kit, and it's filled with chatch for every conceivable occasion, for adults and kids alike.

I carry tire pressure gauges for schmoozing at service stations. I buy them for about ten cents on the dollar. Every time I drive into a service station, oil change shop, or car wash—whether it's a place I frequent or not—I give the attendant or mechanic a tire gauge, because I know that mechanics appreciate practical things.

I also found an array of Allen wrenches at a rummage sale. I couldn't use them, but they were only a buck and a half for four pounds of different-sized wrenches. So I bought them—all of them! I gave them to a mechanic in my hometown who helps me during his off-hours and who occasionally lends me things I need. He was amazed to see the wrenches. His first question was "Where in the world did you get these?" Then he opened his tool case and showed me that he owned only three Allen wrenches. No wonder he was thrilled to see them. This is an example of a perfect gift, bought on impulse, that will be appreciated and remembered for a long time.

I was lucky enough to be on the receiving end of a Million Dollar Chatch Schmooze. The Florida lottery was up to some ridiculously high amount, like 180 million dollars, and made the news every day. John Horwitz, a salesman who supplies my company purchased one hundred lottery tickets and randomly handed them out to my co-workers. When he gave me a ticket, he said, "If you win this, it's all yours. Good luck." I remembered thinking that if I were to win the 180 million dollars, not only would I give him half and pay his taxes, but when he got old, I'd go to his house every day to cover his legs with a blanket. Inspired by this schmooze, I now buy reams of lottery tickets for special occasions, and my friends get a shot at becoming millionaires, all for a buck-a-pop. For my near and dear friends, I enclose a lottery ticket in every birthday card I send them.

Other giveaways include McDonald's gift certificates, movie theater passes, local video store certificates, and passes for car washes. If you give away a handful of certificates (or even one), you'll feel great, because the person you give it to will feel appreciated and acknowledged.

Giving is an important part of friendship. That's why it's a good policy never to enter a host's house empty-handed. It doesn't matter if you bring cut flowers (the gift that's dead and keeps dying), food, wine, or any silly trinket. Personalized gifts like towels, foodstuffs, or wine with personal labels are particularly fun items to give away. If you're stumped for an idea, send a fruit basket a few days before you arrive.

Make the chatch you give memorable. Instead of presenting the host with a philodendron, bring a plant that bears fruit, such as a strawberry barrel or a single tomato plant. That way, when they are enjoying the fruit, they'll be thinking of you. (WARNING: Do *not* give away pets or non-fruit bearing plants as chatch. This piece of advice comes from a wise woman of many pithy sayings—my mother—who said, "Never bring home anything that eats or can't be eaten.")

Don't exclude chatch for the kids, even it it's only a thirty-five cent bottle of soap bubbles. The kids have fun blowing bubbles, and the parents will remember your kind gesture. Or bring a disposable camera, take pictures during the day, have them developed, and send them to your host as a thank-you gift. A long-lasting chatch is a sign-in guest book. It'll stay in the household forever, and because you'll be the first to sign it, they'll always remember you.

When you are buying chatch, think carefully about the person that you are buying it for and consider what they might need or be collecting. Make sure that the amount you spend is appropriate for the level of the relationship, otherwise the gift has the potential of becoming a burden for them. Bearing chatch is not about looking for reciprocation. These gifts are meant to be given freely, since bearing chatch is about being kind, not about being repaid in-kind.

With that said, if you give freely, many times your kindness will be reciprocated, and chatch can open doors, sometimes literally. Let me give you an example. Two days before I wrote this chapter, I had a job at the Oneida Casino in Green Bay, Wisconsin, headlining with my comedy act (I'm one of the better paid unknowns). Since Green Bay borders beautiful Door County (which is the finger sticking out of Wisconsin into Lake Michigan), I took my family along for a vacation. The next day, we took off for Sister Bay in Door County. We were going to do all the tourist things...fish, go on the bike trails, etc. But that afternoon, I realized that

HOLIDAYS TO REMEMBER

National Secretary's Day

Mother's Day
(Don't assume everyone is a mother...)

Father's Day

Grandparents' Day

Teachers Appreciation Day

---

being as far as we were from home, I would have to find lodging in Door County. I asked a local what was nice, and he told me the name of a beautiful resort condominium with Jacuzzis in the rooms, a game room, indoor and outdoor swimming pools—the works. I called and inquired how much for the night. Mind you, this was their peak season in mid-August, so I wasn't surprised when the clerk's reply was $179. I thanked him, and we went on with our go-carting and miniature golf.

Just before supper, we decided we had better settle down to some lodging. I walked into the very posh place about which I had inquired on the phone, walked up to the clerk, and said, "Would you like to have your joke for today?"

Nine out of ten people who are asked this question reply, "Boy, do I need a joke today." Luckily, this clerk was one of the nine.

I'm sure I don't need to remind you that you should never use anything but a G-rated joke in a situation like this. So I said, "Do you know what the snail said as he rode on the turtle's back?" And he asked, "What?" And I said (in a high-pitched voice with all the glee I could muster), "Wheeeeee!!!"

Then I said, "Okay, good-looking, this is yours." I produced a small teddy bear wearing a T-shirt that read "You're No. 1." (I had found these in the Oriental Traders' catalogue for about 16 cents each.) I popped the teddy bear onto the counter and said, "Do you have a rate for a starving artist?" He laughed and said, "Yes," and started filling out the paperwork. When he passed it back to me for my signature, I noticed the rate was under $100 for two bedrooms, a kitchen, foyer, front porch, and Jacuzzi tubs in each bathroom.

When I returned to the car and shared the story with my wife, she gave me the biggest reward of all by saying, "You haven't lost your touch." To me, it was only more living proof that time after time this kind of schmooze works. A little levity, a spark of human kindness, and a lovely measure of chatch.

ASSEMBLING YOUR CHATCH KIT

When you see things you know will make perfect chatch for you, buy them. Don't think about how you will use them, how much it will cost, or how absurd the item may be. If your gut instinct tells you it's a good purchase, then shut off your rational, argumentative self and buy them.

Where can you find great chatch? Rummage sales, going out of business sales, flea markets, dollar shops, toy stores, discount shops, grocery or specialty stores, candy stores, church fairs, catalogs such as The Oriental Trader Co., Inc. (1-800-228-2269) and Dillon Importing, Inc./MG Novelty Co. (1-800-654-3696). A schmoozer's haven is the store that does engraving and will personalize items such as bracelets, pens, plaques, or key chains for you. And if you like making and giving handmade items, learn the crafts of origami or dollar folding, because they are skills that allow you to give chatch on the spot. Things you make personally are always the most highly respected gifts. There is also a wonderful book, *Finding the Perfect Gift: The Ultimate Guide*, by Lisa Hullana and Karl Preson, that can help you find the perfect, unusual gift when you've run out of ideas.

The example I just gave you is one version of the Travel Schmooze, which is one of the best opportunities for chatch-giving. If you travel a lot, as I do, you know that all hotels and motels very quickly begin to look and feel alike. I use the Travel Schmooze to prevent a jaded outlook about traveling from taking hold.

When I check into a hotel, the first thing I say to the desk clerk is, "Hi good-lookin', my name is Aye Jaye, and I'm your willing servant." It's an employee's job to be of service, so they never expect that anyone would want to be of service to *them*. I have found that this comment disarms even the most wired person and lets them see that they are dealing with a friendly human being, not just another demanding customer. It also allows me to see the clerk as a real person rather than as someone who exists solely to satisfy my pressing needs. Continuing along this line of thought, I sometimes say, "As soon as you get me checked in, you can have the rest of the day off." If they respond to this simple statement by sighing and saying "I wish!" then I'll ask them what they would do with a day off. Soon, they're telling me about themselves, and we're laughing and relating in a way that makes our day. We have bonded.

Once, I bought fifty digital watches for two dollars each, and within two months, I had only four left. Before leaving on any trip, I would put a few of the watches in my briefcase. Then, when I checked into each hotel, I'd hand a watch to the desk clerk. I'd explain to them that the watch was theirs to keep, to give away, or to toss, just to watch time fly (bad pun, I know, but it always gets a smile). The result of treating the clerk with such lighthearted respect is usually a better room. They were more than happy to give back to me the only thing they had to give...better service.

Another way schmoozing can make traveling easy and enjoyable is to adopt a bellhop by tipping double the amount you ordinarily would upon arriving. Why do this? It's been said that you can know people by three signs: their temper, their tipping, and their tipping. Any bellhop knows that anyone tipping double the going rate is an experienced traveler, so he is willing to give his all. He becomes your personal coach, the guy-in-the-know, the towner, someone who gets you back on the freeway, gives you directions to the closest mall where you can get film and bottled water at human prices, gets you the best deal on rental cars, steers you away from the restaurant that is famous for its chicken ptomaine, tells you that Hubcap World isn't all that it's pumped up to be, and informs you which neighborhoods or streets to avoid.

If you pay special attention to the maids when you're traveling, you'll discover that the maids pay special attention to you. I always leave a dollar on each pillow that someone slept on, and when I come into the room, I often find that the maid has left me flowers, ice in the bucket, or extra mints on the pillow. After that, I have no problem asking for feather pillows or extra towels. Incidentally, I have never had anything stolen from my room.

No matter where you travel, or how long you stay, you can always build positive relationships with hotel staff through the smart art of schmoozing.

Start preparing a Chatch Crash Kit for your car today, and be sure to put something in it for everyone. There's no secret formula for bearing chatch and no end to the possibilities of finding new ways to share it. I'm always looking for new opportunities to spread cheer and goodwill, and I hope you will too. I guarantee that by the end of a day of schmoozing with chatch, you'll realize that you have received double the amount that you've given. If all you got with your gift of chatch was a pleasant smile and a smoother transaction, you've just enjoyed a win—win! Because...

When you come bearing chatch, the gift you really bear is YOU!

THINGS TO KEEP IN YOUR CHATCH KIT

- lottery tickets
- coloring books
- kids' bubble blowing necklace
- crayons
- emergency greeting cards for all occasions
- key chains with tiny flashlights
- kazoos
- inexpensive wristwatches
- bags of wrapped candy, such as root beer barrels, butterscotch, toffee

- four plastic raincoats
- hangover kit
- first aid kit
- corkscrew with bottle opener
- tape measure
- small collapsible umbrella
- hide-a-key box with magnet
- car gas caps with compartment for key and money
- bubble gum

CHAPTER THREE

THE "MAKE WHAT YOU SAY, PAY" SCHMOOZE

Leave Them Wanting You to Go on, Instead of Wanting You to Go

A theatrical booking agent hears about a talking horse on a farm in northern Wisconsin. He drives up to the pasture, and one of the horses comes up to the fence and says, "You looking for somebody?" The guy says, "Oh my God! Yes, I'm looking for you. You're really a talking horse!" The horse says, "Yup. I'm fluent in four languages, I'm familiar with all the classics, I recite William Shakespeare, and nine years ago, I won the Kentucky Derby." The booking agent says, "That's great! I'm going up to the farmhouse, and I'm going to buy you from your owner. You're going to have a great life in show business, you'll be on Letterman and Leno, you'll have a clean, clean stall and all the oats you can eat." The horse says, "That's cool with me, man, go for it." So the booking agent knocks on the farmer's door. The farmer says, "Can I help you?" Agent: "Do you own that wonderful talking horse out there in the pasture?" Farmer: "Yeah. Why? Did he give you that B.S. about winning the Kentucky Derby nine years ago?"

The point of the story? Even a talking horse isn't worth much if he's a chronic liar.

Schmoozers know what their words are worth. What you say is what tells other people who you are, so words are very, very important. The first words you utter in any interaction instantly convey your intentions, your mood, your sense of self, and the respect—or disrespect—you feel for others. A terse, snide, or derogatory opening is certain to short circuit the current in any conversation. The result will be resistance or a blown fuse, and you won't be very likely to get what you need. Schmoozers are circuit makers, not circuit breakers. They know how to say the right thing so that they'll eventually hear the right thing in return.

The best way to show someone you respect them—and that you're treating them as a person, not just a cog in society's machine—is to address them by name. When I'm introduced to someone, I repeat their name to myself five times so I won't forget it. Then I rhyme it with something and think of someone else who also has that same name to help me remember. When I say good-bye to my new friend, I always use his/her name, such as: "Nice meeting you Bruton, I won't forget it." You'd be surprised what a difference it makes.

If you ever catch yourself with egg on your face because you have forgotten a name (and you can't fake out of it), say, "Please forgive me, I suffer from an affliction called 'sometimers,' which is like Alzheimer's, just not as advanced." This should give some levity to the situation at hand. But it only works once, so next time, you'd better not goof again!

A good goal in any verbal exchange is to connect with the other person and "get them on your side" within the first thirty seconds of interacting. The best way to have them acknowledge you is to acknowledge them first. Ask them a question that will allow them to answer in a positive way and nod their heads "yes" instead of "no." See if you can get them to smile, or better yet, laugh. As Victor Borge so brilliantly said, "Laughter is the shortest distance between two people." (That's the only way one should ever be "short" with people.)

If you approach every situation with the attitude that whomever you are talking with is going to do the right thing for you and is going to want to help you, you are already setting yourself up for success. To ensure that the relationship is going to start out on the right foot, begin each encounter with at least two Talking Schmoozes. Here's my favorite: "Hi good-lookin'. I just walked in the door, took one look at you, and said to myself 'You aren't paid enough nor are you appreciated enough,' because it's apparent to me that you know more than anybody else. You just have that look about you, and it's obvious to me that everybody likes you...and anybody who doesn't is just jealous. Now, can you help me with this?"

Does the person know they are being schmoozed? Of course. But the people just before you in line probably weren't kind, and now you come along, and you brighten their day. Maybe they'll turn to a co-worker and say, "See, I told you so!" or they'll ask you to repeat the schtick in front of a friend or their boss. Trial and error will help you find the openers or one-liners most suited to your personality and temperament. It doesn't matter if you're not naturally witty or spontaneous—like any skill, all it takes is practice. And whether you believe it or not, the person, who you just complimented and told "everybody likes you and anybody who doesn't is just jealous," though they know you've been schmoozing them, agrees with you completely.

Now, you may think that approaching someone you don't know—man or woman—with the words, "Hi-ya good-lookin', how ya doin' partner?" or "Good-lookin', what can I do for you?" are insincere forms of flattery that serve no purpose other than personal amusement. You may even think, "That's too brash or politically incorrect" or "I could never say that!" To those retorts, I would respond, "Why not?" Based on my experience with this disarming comment, I guarantee that if you say "Hello handsome" or "Howdy gorgeous" to ten people, nine of the ten will give you a broad smile. A few people might give you a look that conveys "Are you talking to me?" some might ask you if you've left your glasses at home, and occasionally, one or two will play along and return the compliment. One time, a co-worker of the person I was dealing with overheard my comment and, even though it wasn't addressed to her, said "Thank-you."

I make it a point to use this kind of verbal schmooze, particularly with people who are in work situations that require lots of contact with the public, since they have a greater need for a kind, funny, or unusual comment. These places include: the Department of Motor Vehicles, the parking lot at the ball park, the drive-through window at the bank, and the toll booths on the highway. Workers in these places are often treated poorly or dismissed because other people look down at jobs they consider unimportant. We're always ready with a curse or dirty look when things go wrong, but how often do we recognize a worker's efficiency and competence when everything runs smoothly? The important thing is to recognize that most people believe that their job is important. If you sincerely acknowledge the importance of it, not only will it not cost you anything, but who knows, you may get a special favor in return.

So it's my goal to try and brighten the day of every person who works in one of these jobs. This means treating them with respect, courtesy, warmth, and a true understanding that they are more than their "role" or their "position."

Once, when I was at the Department of Motor Vehicles, I encountered a woman employee who looked like she hadn't smiled in so long that I was afraid if I made her smile, a piece of her cheek would fall off. She had just jumped all over the man in front of me for not writing the proper information on the correct lines of his license form. In fact, she sent him to the back of the line to fill out the form all over again. But I decided to approach her as I would any other person I'd encounter in this kind of situation. After all, I thought, "There is no obstacle too great, no person too stiff for a schmoozer." With a big smile, I looked at her and said, "Good-lookin', can you help me with this?" She paused for a moment, looked up at me, and gave me a very warm smile—and her cheek didn't fall off! Then she struck up an animated conversation about the weather and was very pleasant. I had not completed some of the lines on my form, but instead of yelling, she handed me a pen, and I filled them out and was on my way. The non-schmoozer was a loser since he was still standing in line when I left.

Once you've mastered the Talking Schmooze, you'll have a powerful tool to finesse those awkward or dire situations you may occasionally find yourself in. For example: You're already running late for an important date, but your car is making terrible sounds you've never heard before. You pull into a service station, fearing the worst, which is hearing the attendant say, "You're not going anywhere with that car tonight." It's now seven minutes to five, and you can tell that the mechanic wants to go home. How are you going to encourage him to want to help you with your problem? Pleading, begging, whining, or threatening won't work. Given this scenario, what would you do?

What I did in this situation (since it really did happen to me) was break into song. I sang "You're the top, you're the Tower of Pisa; you're the top, you're the Mona Lisa; you're an old Van Gogh, you're a big so and so; you're a mop"—then I dropped down on one knee for the big finish—"but coming from the bottom, you're the top! I'll sing, I'll dance, I'll take off my pants, just please fix my car."

The mechanic laughed and said, "You can keep your pants on—I'll see what I can do with your car."

Was I schmoozing him? You bet I was, but he was smiling and at least willing to investigate that irritating clang that was coming from under the hood. It would have been much easier for him to say, "I'm sorry, but I won't be able to look at it until the morning, you'll have to leave the car here or come back tomorrow." Schmoozing didn't hurt him, and it certainly didn't harm me.

If you can't sing, then break into a Shakespearean sonnet, or a limerick, or offer to run and get the guy a sandwich, but always do something that will please him so that he will want to please you.

Another example of pleasing vs. pleading occurred while I was trying to get onto the main field of County Stadium during the pre-game for the Milwaukee Brewers so I could sing the national anthem. I thought parking close to the stadium would be a simple matter, but since the parking attendants are constantly being harassed by folks who insist they have a "legitimate excuse" for needing to park near the stadium instead of three miles away from it, they are always on guard. They get grumpy and don't want to hear any excuses. Still, I assumed that I'd be able to park where I needed because Dick Hackett, the director of PR for the Brewers, had given me the OK. However, the parking attendant who stopped me (who was king-of-the-realm in his orange coveralls) said, "Sorry, dat Dick Hackett ain't got no 'tority down here." I thought I was sunk. Then I noticed the guy's name sewn on his jacket. I said to him, "I'm supposed to find Ralph. He knows where I'm supposed to park." He responded, "I'm Ralph." I whipped out a key chain flashlight—one of my favorite chatch giveaways—and handed it to him, thinking he'd be able to use it at night games. I said, "I was told by Mr. Hackett that you handle the special events better than anybody else and that I should make sure to find you. Could you help me out please?" Ralph, now realizing his importance, found me a great parking space.

Later, I related the story to the Dick (who now knows that he has no "'tority" in the parking lot). And in case I might be needing his services again, I sent Ralph a note thanking him for a job well done and cc:'d Dick so that Ralph would see just how high up his kindness would be recognized.

Just as your handwriting and your signature are unique to you, your style of phrasing or praising should also be unique to you. What's important is that you feel comfortable. It's perfectly OK to create a "saying" or line that you use repeatedly (unless you use it with the same person—then it gets old very quickly). It might even become your signature line. Bartenders are famous for having their own way of greeting customers. Some will address a patron as "Your Honor," "My Lord or Lady," "Doctor," "Boss," or even "'Cuz." The bartenders become known for their style of service, and patrons clamor to be served by them because of their humor and playfulness.

Finding your schmoozing style or your signature lines may take time, but don't be afraid to experiment. The following are some short lines that I sometimes say to put people at ease. If you feel like borrowing one or more, be my guest. Maybe they will spawn an idea for your own conversational ice breakers. A word of caution: sexual harassment is in the eye of the beholder—always be both politically and sexually correct, and choose your statements and audience with care.

- "Just for that, take the rest of the day off with pay. Go to the mall, buy shoes."

- "From your lips to God's ears."

- "You're a god, not a man." (Or: "You're a goddess, not a woman.")

- "And how proud your parents must be."

- "I believe in you."

- "I'll never say no to you."

- "You should run for president."

- "The first time I ever saw you do that was like the first time I ever drew a breath, and if I ever said that before, may I be paralyzed on my right side." (Then stick your right arm out straight and stiff, and squint the right side of your face.)

- "You're a tractor *and* a trailer."

- "Everybody likes you, and everybody that doesn't like you is just jealous. And we don't even like those people."

- "If you never win another race, I'll still be betting on you."

- "If you do that for me, I will give you my first born child, I will come to wherever you are when you're old and cover your legs with a blanket, and get you a long spoon to put farina on the ceiling with, and take you for long walks in the park where the young men/women jog."

- "You're *mas* cool."

- "Just thanking you falls short of my feelings."

- "Does Hollywood know about you?"

- "Must be nice to get to pick your parents."

- "Ok, you guys win. You're the best looking couple I've seen today."

- "That's why you make the big money."

- "Are we related and you were stolen by gypsies as a child?"

- "Nobody can do that better than you."

- "When I grow up, I want to be just like you, only younger."

- "God bless you and everybody you hug."

- "Give me a copy of your diet."

- "That was splendeloquent."

- "That's got to be a God-given talent."

- "How many years did you go to graduate school to do that?"

- "I've talked to the Governor, you're getting out of here."

- "You're but 4—but 4 you we wouldn't be here."

- "You are obviously having a good hair day."

- "I drink to the health of my enemies' enemies."

- "Good name _____, won't forget it!"

- "If my I.Q. were one point lower, I'd be (current Vice President)."

- "God bless the hands that made the food and the hands that labored for it."

- "I love you, don't die, don't even get sick." (I say this in the mirror every morning.)

- "Your stock just went up with me another point."

- "I'll always shield you from shame."

- "Please forgive me, I have sometimers—it's like Alzheimer's, but not as advanced."

- "And woe be to the wicked and whomever takes your name in vain."

- "I love and respect you, and I'll always be here to protect you."

- "Are you free to travel?"

- "Well, your kids are good-looking, so they're going to be rich."

- "Excuse me, your child is incurably cute."

- "Any messages? I never get any, so could you make something up?"

- "You're so good-looking that if I weren't married, I'd let you reject me."

- "No matter how rich and famous you get, the size of your funeral will depend on the weather."

- "There's nothing I wouldn't do for you, and there's nothing you wouldn't do for me, and we go through life doing nothing for one another."

- "You're good, and you don't charge anything for being good, which means you're good for nothing, and I appreciate that."

The last two comments always get a laugh and are also good P.S.'s for letters, but only if you say them as if you don't realize they're malapropisms. In the long run, it will be worth your while, for more often than not, you'll end up hearing, "You've made my day. Nice talkin' with ya."

One more schmooze to try, just for you:

This is almost the most fun you can have alone. When you're flying and get off the plane and come through the gangway into the airport, call out excitedly, "Hi everybody, I'm back!" When they realize nobody's there to greet you, they'll all laugh, and a few of them will say "hi" and "welcome back." Put your head down and say, "Ah, you don't care, there's a lot of hate in the world." And even down at the baggage pickup, people will still come up to you and pat you on the back and say that they care. I guarantee!

I did this at LAX in Los Angeles, and a lovely African-American woman in a white hat and dress stood up and yelled, "Son!" She took me totally by surprise, but I instantly replied, "Mom!" She put her arms out, and I ran into them. Both ends of that concourse gave us a standing ovation for at least three minutes. Her husband, the thinnest man I ever saw in a white suit, was on the floor laughing so hard, for a moment there I thought we were going to lose him. It was my second favorite moment in my life. If you're reading this "MOM," thanks a lot!

CHAPTER FOUR

THE "MAKE IT HAPPEN" SCHMOOZE

Put Up and Set Up

Sometimes life's magical moments happen spontaneously, and that's great. But you can't count on good luck all the time. ("Good luck" is what they say to you in a casino just before they take your money.) If you remain open to the possibility that magical moments can actually be manufactured, your life will be filled with a lot more specialness.

The "Make It Happen Schmooze" is a way of "creating spontaneity." The best way to explain is to give you a couple of examples:

My wife was going scuba diving for the first time, and I wanted her to have fun. It can be scary going deep underwater with tanks on your back, so I tried to think of some way to make her relax. I asked a couple we were going to be diving with, Pete Aasen and Winney, to be my accomplices. That morning, we fried ten silver dollars in a pan to make them appear old. Then when we were diving, as Pete and Winney swam ahead of us, they randomly dropped the silver dollars. When my wife discovered the coins at the bottom of the lake, instead of being worried about her breathing tanks, she spent all her nervous energy exploring the depths and looking for more sunken treasure. She thoroughly enjoyed the dive and since then has become a master diver. She's the best scuba diving partner I've ever had.

The most difficult part of the dive was after we surfaced. I had to use all my concentration to keep a poker face as I told her how disappointed I was that I didn't find a single silver dollar. (I might be in hot water when she reads this, because she'll learn that not only did I plant her buried treasure, but that there were ten silver dollars, not just the nine that she discovered. I hope she doesn't insist that I find the last coin.)

Another example:

One day in Paris, when my colleague M & M, Mary Miller (a young version of Liz Taylor), and I had a day off, we went to Montmartre and there met a friendly English-speaking couple. We exchanged names, bought one another drinks, and had a wonderful afternoon. By accident, we met them again the next day on the Champs Élysées. We laughed at the great coincidence of meeting again, especially in a city as large as Paris.

I began to think about how incredible the odds would be of meeting a third time. When M & M went to the rest room, I shared my idea with the couple about the possibility of "accidentally meeting" one more time. They mentioned that in two days they were traveling to Versailles, and so we secretly planned to meet again at two o'clock at the statue of Louis XIV. When my colleague returned, we all said good-bye and laughed again about the wonderful coincidence.

On Saturday, during the train ride to Versailles, I began to set the stage for our rendezvous by talking about coincidences, perfect timing, and how mysteriously connected we all are to each other. After buying our tickets to go inside the Palace of Versailles, we walked around the outside while I kept watching the time and hoping that the couple remembered our plan to meet. When we walked up to the statue, they were sitting there, looking innocent. Of course my colleague was astounded at this third, miraculous "coincidence." We laughed and had a good time and didn't reveal our secret until dinner. When we told my friend that our meeting had been pre-arranged, she screamed "What?" with mock dismay, but she loved it. None of us will ever forget that spring in Paris.

The key to the "Make It Happen" Schmooze is to think ahead. Ask yourself, "What could I do by phoning, making advance arrangements, or having a surprise set up prior to an event or meeting?"

For the people on the receiving end of your schmooze, especially if your idea is a surprise, it is going to seem as though the events happened "by magic." You will be the only one who knows differently. And ideally, it should be that way. Your schmoozing should not call attention to itself, and you should not point out to people how wonderful you are for thinking of them. That would defeat the purpose of schmoozing, since bragging makes you, and not others, the focus. You have to take the attitude of magicians who never reveal the secrets to their magic tricks because it would take away all the fun.

It's important to remember, though, that there is a difference between a "Make It Happen Schmooze" and a practical joke. Practical jokes tend to make the recipient the "butt" or target of the joke, and the feelings that are usually associated with receiving such a joke are anger, embarrassment, disgust, or revenge. All a person wants to do is get back at those who pulled the "fast one" on them. You must always be sensitive to the personality and level of jocularity of the person being schmoozed. You are not schmoozing so that *you* can feel good or get a chuckle; you are schmoozing because you want the other person to feel special, acknowledged, or uplifted.

Let's look at some specific ways to schmooze for surprise...

Restaurants are the perfect place to make it happen. Whether you're there for a business luncheon, a social gathering, or a romantic evening, you can always add your special top-spin touch to make dining out even more pleasant.

If I know that I am going to dine with a large group of people, I will phone the restaurant and prepay for a tray of appetizers that will be ready as soon as our party is seated. I make a request that when the hors d'oeuvres are served, the server announces that they are "compliments of Aye Jaye." I do this not to gain a round of applause (which sometimes happens), but to make sure that no one is worrying throughout dinner about who is going to foot the bill for this unexpected treat.

If you are being treated to dinner in a city other than your own, make sure to learn the name of the restaurant where you will be eating. Then, if you can, phone ahead and chat with the maitre d' to see if she or he

MAKING GOOD THINGS HAPPEN

Here are some other special items that can be personalized for a make it happen effect. A little personal effort on your part will go a long way:

- fortune cookies
- horoscopes
- an autographed photo of their favorite celebrity
- a set of coins from the year of their birth
- personalized stationery
- numismatists have silver coins and bars for all occasions with

blank spaces for personal engraving
- personalized pencils
- etched glasses
- cement garden stone with their last name
- brass name plate for their desk or entryway at home
- coffee cup with their picture on it

would be willing to be your accomplice for a "Make It Happen" Schmooze. All that is required of them is to greet you by name as if you are a regular customer, to inquire about your family, your health, and well-being. Your hosts will be amazed that you're so well-known, even in a city that's not your home.

A promoter friend of mine who owns Bell Ambulance, one Jimmy Lombardo, has a great schmooze. Every time someone who's special to him gets some favorable press, he takes it to a trophy store and has it embossed on a plaque. Then he presents it to the person as a gift from his company. Nice schmooze!

The Birthday Schmooze is another good one for restaurants. Whenever I go out to dinner with friends or clients, I try to discover, (without being discovered) if it's someone's birthday. If no one has a birthday on the day we are going to dine, I select one person from our group who I think might enjoy celebrating their birthday. During the meal, I sneak away (usually by saying I have to use the little boys' room) and talk to the waiter or waitress. I let them know that we are celebrating a birthday and ask if they would bring over a piece of birthday cake so we can sing "Happy Birthday" to the honored guest. Depending upon the restaurant, the staff sometimes joins in the singing.

In all the time I've been doing this, I've never had one person deny it was their birthday. Everyone smiles and is very gracious. You might want to try a song other than the traditional "Happy Birthday." Or, if you see that your "birthday" person is enjoying the attention, after everybody sings the usual version, propose to sing it twice ("Happy happy birthday birth-day to to you you..." etc.). If you lead the song, everyone will catch on—including other patrons within earshot.

If your group is spending an evening at a comedy club, write on a slip of paper the name of the person that you've chosen to have the birthday, and ask one of the staff to give it to the comic before the show. Any good comic usually has a birthday, anniversary, bachelor or bachelorette, or divorce bit that he or she likes to do, and it will make the evening quite special for the person who gets the comic's attention. If you send $5 and tell the comic to get a drink, he'll really work them over for you. A great way to finish the evening is to present a little "birthday" gift to the person along with the words, "This is for you, for being such a great sport. Happy Birthday!" This will ensure that the person feels positive about having been singled out, rather than feeling embarrassed or like the target of a cruel hoax.

The "Make It Happen" Schmooze is also a great way to truly make it happen when you're angling for something important. One of my favorite ways to schmooze my boss, a client, or a potential client when we've scheduled an important meeting is to bring in the daily newspaper—in which I will have previously placed an ad that reads, "John DeSalvo (or the client's name) impresses others with his great judgment, good looks, good taste, and obvious intelligence in accepting this offer." Then, during the meeting, I'll open the paper and say, "Look, I know you'll see it this way. After all, it's in the newspaper." I'll turn to the page, circle the ad, and let him read it. It's at least good for a laugh. He'll know he's being schmoozed, but just knowing I took the time to plan ahead may influence him to make the decision in my favor.

Here's another way to get in the good graces of your clients or boss. Discover their interests, and then buy them tickets to a concert or game or event they'll enjoy. Buy four of the best tickets you can, giving two to your target and keeping the other two yourself. At the event, guess who you are sitting next to and getting next to? Your boss or client will be impressed that you thought of them, and they'll probably be excited to share their expertise or interest with you. Who knows, you might discover that you really do like opera, bagpipe music, or yodeling.

I've saved my two favorite "Make It Happen" Schmoozes for last, both of which are tailored for weddings. I call the first one the "best table" gag. The next time you're at a wedding banquet with a group of people you don't know, first introduce everybody at the table to one another. Then tell them, "We need to be the best table at this function. When I count to three, let's all laugh as hard as we can—then we'll repeat it every ten minutes." You do become the most popular table at the event. Everyone wishes they were sitting with you. And because you have the common bond of your inside joke, the conversation will flow at your table, truly making it the best in the room.

Here's the last one. When the guests at a wedding start tapping on their glasses to make the blissful couple kiss, stand up and announce that there will be no more glass tapping. Tell the group that from now on, when you want the couple to kiss, you have to stand up, either singularly or with a group, and sing a song with the word "love" in it. It's a stitch to watch (both at the moment and later, on the video). You're likely to hear people whose voices would shatter glass and a group of intoxicated people trying to be the Supremes ("Stop in the Name of Love"). It is an absolute guarantee that someone will sing the theme from "Love Boat."

The "Make It Happen" Schmooze says a lot about you. It says you care. It says the person you've taken the time to schmooze is special and important to you. That kind of attention and caring is what builds relationships filled with trust and integrity.

It pays to plan ahead, so put up and set up!

CHAPTER FIVE

IF THE SCHMOOZE FITS, CARE FOR IT

Servicing People in the Trenches

There is a long ago and probably forgotten comic from Louisiana called the "Lovely Brother Dave Gardner." He once told me that heaven and hell are basically the same. In both places, there is great gourmet food (and sushi), but everyone has these long spoons tied to their arms. They can scoop up the food, but they can't put it in their mouths because the spoons are too long. The difference between heaven and hell is that in hell, everyone is starving, but in heaven, they're full and happy as clams because they're feeding one another.

Schmoozing is a way of feeding other people in the hope that eventually, you'll be fed too. I said earlier that schmoozers are more givers than takers. But since one good deed deserves another, if you give enough, then you'll be given things in return.

To make sure the system works for you, you have to tend your personal contacts like a bed of flowers. You have to plant seeds early so you can reap a good harvest.

Let me give you an example of how to "service" your contacts:

There's a fellow I know who works at the local ballpark. Remember, baseball is a seasonal game. It's nearly impossible to get hold of this guy when the Brewers are in the heat of the season. But during December, nothing's going on, and I figure the guy is bored and lonely. That's why I always give him a call then. I tell him that I realize the rest of the world has forgotten about him temporarily, but I still care. I let him know that I'm still out there and I'm still his friend. He always laughs like hell, and sure enough, when April rolls around, he's not too busy to help find me good seats to Opening Day.

Another example of how giving leads to being given:

One time when I was flying through Chicago, a number of flights got delayed, and the airport was chaos. I was able to get myself rebooked through my Travel-Rite agent, but I watched the airport concierge taking care of other disgruntled customers. He stood there like a traffic cop at a very busy intersection, getting the entire matter settled in no time at all. I was very impressed, so I went up and had a conversation with him. We exchanged business cards, and lo and behold, the next time I had an insurmountable situation at O'Hare, I called upon my good friend, John Renfrow, and he was there to help me. That afternoon, I wrote to the CEO of the company to tell him what a great person he had in place at O'Hare.

The next time I came through the airport, the concierge had obviously done his homework because he met me at the gate to thank me for the nice letter and invited me to the airline lounge during my layover. As we talked, we found out that we shared the hobby of boating. Since that time, we have gotten together for a number of weekend boating trips. It's a win-win situation, because now I choose to use his airline whenever I fly, just on the chance that I might get to see him.

We're schmoozing one another, which is exactly what we should be doing.

Here are some tips for servicing some of your most common contacts in the service industries:

RESTAURANTS

Whenever I go to a new restaurant, the first thing I do is introduce myself to the waiter or waitress. Then I give her a dollar bill folded into a ring with the number one showing on top (you can do this and several other money folding tricks by just calling 1-800-92-MAGIC and asking for the book, "Folding Money #1" for $6 from Abbott Magic). I tell her that she's #1 with me and there's more coming at the end of dinner. After that act, I have never received bad service.

Try this or some other personal greeting. And remember to always tip more than the standard rate. Good tipping brings good luck, but more important, it brings good service. And if you've ever worked in this industry, you already know what I'm talking about.

HOTELS

If you stay at a hotel and have a particularly good experience, get to know the concierge or manager. Then, if a friend of yours is looking for a place to stay, recommend that hotel, and tell your friend to mention your name to the manager when making the arrangements, saying you suggested the place. The next time you have occasion to go back, you might just find yourself with a free suite.

BUSINESS OWNERS

It's the same thing with any kind of business. I've sold four boats for Earl Retzloff, the boat guy in my hometown, by recommending him to acquaintances. Now, Earl no longer charges me for taking my boat out in the fall or putting it back in the water come spring. This was never a spoken deal. I never sent anybody to him expecting a thing until I finally realized he hadn't sent me a bill—and he has assured me I'm never going to get one.

The key is personal relationships. If you're buying a car and there is a name in the title of the dealership, try to meet the person behind that name. Deal with him or her directly. Managers and salespeople may come and go, but the owner is a person you can get to know, who you can stay in touch with. You can depend on them, and let them know that they can depend on you.

To make sure that you keep your garden plot of personal contacts well-tended, do this exercise:

Jot down the people that you have had dealings with over the course of the last year. I'm talking about people who are suppliers to you, people who do things for you, whether you're paying them or not. Your list might include people and organizations like:

- Travel agents
- Hotel clerks
- Rental car agencies
- The boat dealer
- The dry cleaner
- The ticket manager at the local ticket outlet
- Your doctor and dentist and their nursing staffs
- The service manager at the local garage
- The golf pro
- The manager of the ski hill
- The maitre d' at your favorite restaurant
- The fire department
- The librarian
- The motor vehicle registrar
- Your kid's schoolteacher
- If you know what's good for you, don't forget the garbagemen

Now, think of ways to go out of your way to make these people know your appreciation.

Keep in mind that your appreciation doesn't have to cost you a dime. Sometimes just a phone call can do the trick—not a call that leads up to asking a favor, but just a "Hey, howdy, I was thinking of you" phone call. If you make enough of these calls—sincerely—then once in a while when you *do* have to ask for a favor, it's no big deal.

Other ways of servicing your contacts might cost you a little, but not much. How about tomatoes? Yeah, tomatoes. My daughters, Zsajsha and Z'dra, and I plant tomatoes every spring, and in the summer, we always end up giving away a ton of them. Recently, the pump for my well died. The plumber came out to my place to check things out, and he told me the cost of a new pump would be $400, plus labor. We were coming up from the pump house past the garden, and I thought, "Hey, maybe the plumber would like some tomatoes." I asked him, and he enthusiastically said yes, so I filled a bag. Then he noticed I had a pump to water my garden—exactly the same type that I had in the pump house. He suggested that I take the one from the garden, put it in the pump house, and have the other one rebuilt for about $50. For him to switch the pumps would only be $50 in labor. My total savings would be $300. I asked him for his card and said, "Congratulations, you're my new plumber!"

Even if you don't have your own garden, you can still use this method. How about going to a pick-your-own farm or fruit orchard? Pick a few bushels (it's cheap!), and then drive around to some of the people on your list: the doctor's office, the fire station, the police department. You can feel safe knowing that if you ever get in any trouble, the police will remember you as that special person who dropped off a shopping bag full of delicious fresh-picked apples.

CHAPTER SIX

SCHMOOZING
FOR A JOB

Get the Gig

On the late movie last night, I watched the 1960 Academy Award-winning classic, *Bridge over the River Kwai*. In the movie, Japanese General Sato stands on the bridge as he is about to send the English war prisoners off on the impossible task of building a bridge over a quicksand bed in a bug-, snake-, and mosquito-infested jungle. His last words to them are, "In the words of the Emperor, 'be happy in your work.'"

Yeah, right! As if those prisoners could be thrilled about their enslavement.

But if General Sato's advice is all wrong in this situation, at least he's got the right principle. Most of us spend at least 33 percent of our lives working, and we're much better off if we can enjoy what we do. That's why the ability to find a job you like—and then secure that job—is so important.

My father used to say, "Find something you like to do and then find out how to get paid for it." I've let that statement guide my working life, and you can, too.

But before I even get into the best tactics for schmoozing your way into a job you love, I feel duty-bound to make the following statement: *Work for yourself*. If there is any chance at all of your becoming an entrepreneur, or if you have always dreamed of starting a small business, it's high time you put your dreams to the sink-or-swim test. Companies are closing, dumping on their employees, or scamming them out of the benefits once promised. If you work for yourself, it's not an easy path either, but you're guaranteed at least one thing: You'll get along with your boss.

That said, of course not everyone can—or wants to—be self-employed. So let's talk about schmoozing your way into a job.

The first part of the process, like my father said, is figuring out what you want to do. A job should be like a spouse: something you want to learn from and live with for a long time. Too often, people begin with the wrong questions. They ask: What are my skills? How much money could I get? Yes, skills and potential wage are crucial elements of determining what job to seek, but the most important thing is being happy.

So instead, ask yourself this question: When I get a day off, what's the thing I most want to do?

If the answer is staying in bed and reading, then maybe you should consider a job in publishing or as a librarian. If the answer is hiking in the woods, why not look into openings at the National Park Service? If you just can't wait for the weekend to roll around so you can tinker under the hood of your Chevy, then you're a born mechanic.

Do these sound like pipe dreams? They don't have to be. All it takes is a little creativity.

Almost any hobby can be parlayed into an occupation. Here's an example: let's say that your hobby is scuba diving. Snag a job on a treasure boat or with a marine biologist, or working at the Shedd Aquarium in Chicago as a diver. Or, let's say you are a rock hound, and you know somebody who knows somebody, who knows somebody else, who knows about an archeologist who is looking for a helper for a dig in Egypt. Next thing you know, you're at the pyramids! Or if you love to travel, what if there were suddenly a job opening for someone to go out and try all the lush resorts, sample their food and wine, and report back on the quality— now wouldn't that be great? It sure was for my friend Paula, who actually landed that job!

Sometimes the job isn't doing what you love, but it still enables you to do what you love. I knew one woman who more than anything else loved to ski. She went to Vail and got a job as a waitress at one of the ski resorts. She didn't care one way or another about waitressing, but as part of her employee benefits package, she got free skiing all winter long. Needless to say, she was as happy as a snowflake.

Once you've identified what you would *ideally* like to do, it's time to hunt around in the real world and find a job that matches. How are you going to find the right opportunity?

The big buzzwords today are networking and webbing. You can do them on either a small or a big scale. Small: ask your friends and relatives if they know of anyone who is looking for a good person. You're more apt to find a job by asking people around you than you are looking in the classified ads in the newspaper. Somebody knows somebody who's hiring or looking for somebody all the time. You may go through the first three or four people and they won't know anything, and then bingo, you'll hit on somebody that will say, "Yes, I heard about something yesterday," and there you go!

On the bigger scale of networking, you are truly keeping your ear to the ground. You are putting out feelers to find out if there's a fly in your web. And this means getting on the phone and doing your phone work, trying to land yourself in the job you're looking for. Headhunters (AKA, human resource firms) can also be good starting points. In most cases, you don't have to pay these people. They are generally paid by the employer who is looking for a specific talent.

One tool that you have available now that we didn't when I was a kid is the World Wide Web. There is tons of information about specific and general job topics out on the Internet. Some sites will even let you post your resume for potential employers to read.

OK. You've figured out what you want to do, and you've identified a job that seems right. Now, the hard part: Landing the job.

A friend of mine who works in the industry of getting workers back into jobs has a degree in this field and tells me that job hunting in today's market is—and I quote—"50 percent skill and 50 percent schmooze." I was thrilled to hear that.

My first advice for schmoozing your way into a job: Remember that doo-doo runs downhill. So the closer you can get to the top, and I mean the *very* top, the better chance you'll have of getting the job. I've seen it happen time after time, on golf courses and at cocktail parties: the person who gets a shot at the CEO's ear and schmoozes her winds up with the primo job.

You can never shoot too high. If you want to work in the movies, send a letter—or better yet, a video clip of yourself—to the head of Paramount. Make it something memorable. Make the person at the top know that you're *over* the top and that you'll do anything creative to work for the company.

If and when you get to the interview stage is when your schmoozing skills really come into play. Here are some things people look for when they're hiring and tips to win an interviewer's heart:

APPEARANCE

Neatness really does count, in your personal appearance and in the materials you use to present yourself. Dress appropriately. Go ahead and spend the few extra bucks to have your resume printed on high-quality paper;

the cost is nothing compared to the salary you'll pull in once you get the job. If there's an application to fill out and you have a problem with penmanship, see if you can take the paperwork home with you and type it out, then send it back. And a special Aye Jaye trick of the trade: Paper clip a piece of candy to the application when you return it (butterscotch and toffee are the winners). Sweetness begets sweetness!

EAGERNESS

A mistake too many people make in interviews is to be mealy-mouthed and shy. They think they don't have the right to ask for the job, so they just timidly wait and see if it will be offered. You'll be much more impressive if you're eager. Tell the personnel manager, "Hey, I'm the one you want. I give you my personal guarantee right now that I can do this job better than anybody else you've had apply for it today. Help me out here. Help me get this job. I will be eternally grateful to you."

That kind of talk usually gets the personnel person excited, especially if whoever applied before you was blasé during their interview. You'll shine in comparison.

Another sentence employers like to hear is, "I'm not going anywhere. I plan to stay in this area and am looking to make my future with this company. I like your product, your plant, your office, etc." Even if the person who filled out the application before you was a tad more qualified, you've let the hirers know that you can't be beat in terms of commitment and longevity. That just may be the thing that will outweigh other factors and land you the job.

CONNECTION

A great schmooze to do when you're being interviewed, especially if you have the opportunity to be in the interviewer's office, is to find something of common interest, like a picture of her fishing or perhaps her children. Tell her about the last fishing trip you took and the huge walleye you reeled in. Find a common bond that lets you start talking on a human level, person-to-person instead of interviewer-to-interviewee. Turn the tables and ask her questions about herself—she's been in the asker position all day, so she'll be happy for a change of pace.

If you don't have the opportunity to see the interviewer's office, see if you can find something on her person, such as a ring, pin, or tie clasp to comment on and ask about. "That's a great ring," you can say. "Has it been in your family a long time?" It also never hurts to offer compliments, especially humorous ones. Try this one: "Is there a chance that I can get a copy of your diet so I can get a head of hair like you have?" (If the interviewer's a man, make sure he has the hair!)

POSITIVE ATTITUDE

When asked why you left your last job, stay away from "sour grapes," even if you have them. Avoid talking negatively about your ex-employer, because if you do, your potential employer can't help but imagine you talking the same way about him someday down the road. Put a positive spin on things: explain that your reason for seeking this new job is to advance yourself, to learn more, and that you've always liked this type of work and have been waiting for this opportunity.

CONFIDENCE

As with any schmoozing you do, you must be confident when you're angling for a job. People are like dogs—they can smell fear. Make sure that you have a bounce in your step and a smile on your face. Make sure you really feel that you can do the job, because if you do, it will show. Go in and be as schmoozingly charming as you can.

When you're being interviewed, you have nothing to lose by making guarantees. For example, say, "I guarantee I'm the person that you want for this position." Use a sentence like, "I come to work to go to work, and I'm looking forward to learning with you and growing with you if given the chance."

In my lifetime, I have hired hundreds of people and have interviewed at least four times that number. And I have hired the guaranteeing person every single time, because that person is telling me she is committing herself, that she is ready and willing to go to work and to work hard. She's telling me she will give me an honest day's work for an honest day's wage, and 95 percent of the time, I have been right to choose that person.

I always hire the person who makes it clear she's going to love her work, because I remember what my father used to say about getting paid for what you love. Loving your job is the best thing that can happen to you, because it's not at all like having to go to work.

In the words of one of my very own heroes:

"Early to bed, early to rise, work like hell, and advertise."

—Ted Turner

CHAPTER SEVEN

SCHMOOZING THE BOSS

Take It from the Top

There's a great story about a boss who calls the temp agency looking for a computer operator. The person at the agency says, "Sorry, but no one's available. Old buffalo butt Farina has used them all up."

"Do you know who you're talking to?" asks the boss.

Phone voice: "No."

"This is CEO Farina."

"Oh. Well, do you know who this is?"

Boss: "No, I do not."

"Well then good-bye buffalo butt!"

If you've followed my advice in the previous chapter and schmoozed your way into the job you want—great! Congratulations! But the schmoozing doesn't stop once you're in the door. If you want to stay happy in your job and advance as far as possible, you need to schmooze the person who can help (or hurt) you the most: your boss.

Here's my Top Ten list for ways to "take it from the top":

#1. Be a stockholder

If possible, buy into the company that you work for. This shows that you care, that you're playing the game, and that your commitment is far greater than that of just a "worker bee." If the boss knows you have a personal stake in the future of the company, she can be sure that you'll be hardworking and loyal. Have "stockholder" printed on your business card, along with the year you started with the company. Everyone who sees the card will know that you believe in the company and the product.

#2. Do your homework

To schmooze your boss, you need to know a little bit about him. In this world of refuge and nephews, where did he come from? Ask him that question, he wants to tell you. Did he inherit the company? Did she work her way up from the Mail Room? Did she steal her position, or did she earn it? Did he start the company himself? Knowing how your boss came to be boss will give you the insight you need as to her perspective.

Next, find out what the boss is interested in. Then do some homework so you can talk about the subject intelligently. Is your boss an avid bridge player? Get a rule book, and practice your shuffling skills. Is she a movie buff? Rent some old Audrey Hepburn films so you can drop references into conversation around the water cooler.

Don't feel guilty about finding a common interest that will allow you to hang out with the boss. Remember that most positions are filled by "top of mind." If you're the one on the boss's mind when the position opens up, you get it. There's nothing wrong with a common interest helping you out. I don't care if it's an acting group, a church choir, golf, or rock collecting. It doesn't matter, simply because being in the right place at the right time—and dumb luck—are still the most important factors in advancement. As my mom would say, "If you hang around long enough, they start to give you stuff."

#3. KEEP IT SUBTLE, THOUGH

Try not to place yourself in situations where you don't belong or don't fit in. If your boss goes to the Greek Orthodox church and you're Jewish, it's probably not necessary to convert. You don't have to join their country club. Yes, you should work to establish personal connections, but the real basis of your schmoozing should be your good work and your company spirit.

#4. DON'T PUSH TOO HARD

If you try to make a connection with your boss but the chemistry is just not there, back away for a while and give it a rest. Abort any further movement in this direction before you are considered a pain in the establishment.

#5. MAXIMIZE YOUR MEETINGS

Have meetings with the boss in places where the distraction level is as low as possible. The most common place for meetings—in a restaurant, over lunch or dinner—is in my opinion the worst. There are too many distractions: the water glass tipping over, the old friend sitting at the next table. Instead, try having your meeting in a car. That's right, a car. What I generally do is tell the other person that we're going to a really good restaurant; it's a long way away, I say, but it's worth it. I pick an establishment at least a forty-five-minute distance from the office. That way, we have an uninterrupted forty-five minutes going and coming, during which we're each other's only company, and we have each other's undivided attention. When we actually get around to the meal, it doesn't matter if there are distractions, and we can enjoy our food without worrying about business.

If you can't get done what you need to get done during a long car trip, you couldn't sell a boat to a drowning man.

#6. KEEP YOUR HEAD UP

A technique I like to use is what I call a "Heads Up Letter." This does not mean being a snitch or telling on your fellow employees. What I am talking about is sending a brief note every once in a while to let the boss know about some new technology you heard of or some practical business tip. Keep it short, sweet, and informative. "I just wanted to give you a 'heads up' on what I heard," is the gist. You'll be surprised at how that kind of note will get you ahead of all the apple polishers and boot lickers around you.

#7. BE THOUGHTFUL

At Christmastime, I thank three people who are responsible for me even having a Christmas. They are my partner of twenty-five years, Roy, my booker, Roz, and my life partner, Annie. On Labor Day, I send my boss a note saying how glad I am to be employed by him. I also send him a birthday card every year and enclose a $1 bill. This cracks him up because he pulls in a six-figure salary, and the last thing he needs is a measly dollar. But believe me, my dollar means a lot to him. Try to think of other ways to let your boss know that you're thinking of her and that you care. Bosses are people, too!

#8. WATCH OUT

Tactfully watch out for the boss. If you feel he's had too much to drink at the office party, you might want to rescue him and drive him home. Make sure he gets to his car safely. These things stay hard in the hearts of the boss. Knowing that he has people around him who he can trust, who have integrity, and who actually care about whether or not he gets home safely means a lot.

#9. CYA: COVER YOUR ASS-ETS

Don't let other people take credit for your work. You don't want to toot your own horn too loud, but one way or another, the boss has got to know that you're responsible for the good work you do. By the same token, don't let anybody leave you hanging as the fall guy for problems that weren't your doing. Again, a "Heads Up Letter" can stop this.

#10. HAVE FUN!

Bosses like to be part of the fun, but are too often kept out of the loop because employees are afraid of being too casual. Don't be insubordinate; know when to keep your place; but in the right time and place, you should be able to share a few yucks with the head honcho.

In sum: Schmooze your boss with your intelligence, your esprit de corps, your integrity, your workmanship, your talent, and your ambition.

If you follow these Top Ten rules, then someday you might just get to be a boss yourself. All the best bosses I've had were expert schmoozers. That's how they got to the top.

If you do eventually get to be the boss, keep these rules in mind: #1) Maintain an even measure of power and benevolence; #2) Treat all your employees as though you might work for them someday; and #3) Remember to enjoy the view from your corner office!

CHAPTER EIGHT

MANAGING WITH SCHMOOZE

Schmoozing Your Team to Schmooze Your Customers

Every decade there are new ideas about management, leadership, and working as teams. Some motivational movements last, and other concepts and theories fall by the wayside when they prove unfeasible in the day-to-day work world. But schmoozing is tried and true, never out of style. Its golden rule of treating others well is at the heart of teams that are not only successful, but happy too.

There are two key aspects to being a manager who schmoozes. First, you must learn to schmooze your co-workers and team members. Second, you must teach your team members to schmooze your clients, vendors, and customers. Think for a moment about how closely these two aspects are related, and you will see the importance of your own schmoozing skills. Quite simply, if you can't schmooze your own team, you can't expect them to be able to schmooze your customers.

An acronym for TEAM for some managers might be, "Treat Everyone As Mediocre." They may see their team members as unable or unwilling to improve their performance either on their own or through training and guidance. But, if you are a leader or a manager and you are discouraged about the way your team is performing, find a new acronym for TEAM—"Treat Everyone As Major." People will perform based on your attitudes and beliefs about them. Treating them with support, praise, and high expectations gives them something to live up to, not to mention a better chance of doing so.

Do an afternoon getaway, like a picnic or a day at the races, or perhaps just an afternoon where everybody brings a dish and you do nothing but sit around and schmooze. Let them know they are special. Note, I didn't say let them *think* they are special. If you don't believe it, don't expect them to.

Whatever your business, you're providing some sort of service to people, even if you're not face-to-face with buyers every day or your product is superior to all others on the market. The service you and your team provide is critical to your success. Think to yourself about each time you have become upset with service you've received, whether it was something minor at a gas station or grocery store, or something major from an airline or hotel. In most cases, it wasn't the product you had a problem with. Rather, it was an employee who upset you and stopped you from going back. As a matter of fact, because of the incident, you may have told a few people, and those few told several more. See how easily the groundswell of a bad reputation can start?

Not everybody is a born schmoozer, but everybody is a born learner. Your training skills, right from your employee's first day on the job, will make the difference in the service your customers receive. Here are a few team-building tips that will help you teach your employees that excellent service is their number one priority.

1. Teach your employees the meaning of schmoozing and the golden rule. Heck, have them read this book.

2. At the job interview, ask questions like, "what was the last beautiful thing that happened to you that made you cry," "when was the last time you volunteered," etc. If they then start working for you, they have already seen that this is a caring, schmoozing, human organization.

3. Only hire people that you feel are warm, friendly, endearing types.

4. Lead by example. If you're the boss, let them know that you are a caring, schmoozing person. A good start is by having an open office to hear both professional and personal problems.

5. Start a department support group.

6. When hiring people, let them know from the start that their wages are paid by your customers.

7. Make sure that in your initial job interviews, you painstakingly take the time to ask the major question, "Do you want this job?" If the response is "yes," say, "Good, because I want you to feel proud of what you're doing and to handle every person you deal with in the very best manner that you can, as if the business were your own."

8. Let employees know they were hired because they displayed their best attitude and that you will settle for no less while they are working for you.

9. Make it standard operating procedure to have all employees introduce themselves and welcome new employees to the team. It will encourage team camaraderie. Also, consider assigning a 'buddy' to the new hire to guide them through the first week, sit with them at lunch, etc.

10. Remember that praise doesn't cost you anything, but it is priceless. The praise you shower on employees today just might be what will help them tomorrow when they encounter an angry or dissatisfied customer. Instead of passing the buck, they'll say, "I will handle it." They'll fix it and turn the situation around—feeling that they want to do it—because the boss taught them how to schmooze people and do the job right.

11. Have your team take seminars on schmoozing topics, such as the one I recently took, taught by Dr. Turo Rapkin with Leadership Center

Midwest, Creators of Individual and Organizational Vitality, 8689 North Port Washington Rd., Suite 103, Milwaukee, WI 53217 (Ph. 414-241-2888). Or sign them up for a Dale Carnegie Course or the Golden Rule of Schmoozing seminars that yours truly offers. Let them know that your company's integrity is on the line and that schmoozing is not to be thought of as either BSing or lying to the customer. You depend on the employee's ability to translate the company's commitment and personality onto the customer—that's why they were hired in the first place.

With your high-quality, schmooze-conscious team in place, be sure to take time out to remind and reemphasize how important it is to schmooze people. Schedule time to let them know that good service and good relations with everyone inside and outside your company will be rewarded:

- Have meetings where employees can share their thoughts on how to improve customer relations.

- Have incentive programs to reward the best ideas.

- Act out service scenarios. Think "outside the circle," use props, exaggerate, and have fun!

- Offer incentives like movie passes, gift certificates, or best parking space for the "Master Customer Schmoozer of the Month."

- Have a "Best Schmooze Contest," complete with a trophy and crowning ceremony.

Schmoozing the members of your team to schmooze others is the most important thing you can do in the world of dreamers and doers. As you have probably experienced, not all teams are successful, since any team is only as good as the individuals who comprise it. Any group can only move as fast as its slowest member, and there will always be a few angry, negative naysayers in any group, dragging it down and squelching ideas without contributing anything of value. Managers and team members who feel as though they are fighting a losing battle tend to moan and groan about the "slugs" and "slackers" they have to work with. This is the worst possible attitude to hold about individuals or teams.

A true team player, like my friend Liz Zak, is a natural schmoozer. Liz's locker at work is filled with candy bars, energy bars, and power snacks for the office workers who have to work late. They know if they take a snack from her locker to replace it the next day. Another team player, Tammy Parish, the famous Ringling clown, always set up a card table in clown alley for anyone working with the circus. On the table were needles and thread, aspirin, liniment, gum, toothpaste, spare change, bandages, and lots of other goodies that one might need in a pinch. Again, everyone knew to later replace anything that they took from the table. Both Liz and Tammy held the value that because everyone is in this life together, why not give a helping hand and make living on this planet a little easier?

Individuals who think this way understand that a team is more than just a few people who work together to accomplish a specific goal. Their view encompasses everyone in their sphere of influence. My tap dancing friend Audrey is a perfect example of someone who sees team playing in a larger context. She will baby-sit for the kids in the neighborhood at very low rates, and as a side benefit, she will teach them how to tap dance while she is sitting for them, free of charge. This living "Mary Poppins" was nominated for a citizen's award for her service to the community. Audrey also knows that what goes around, comes around: her lawn is mowed, her trees are trimmed, and her snow is shoveled for free, plus, she never picks up the tab at the local restaurant. There's a quality of caring and goodness about a person like this that makes you wish they were on your team.

The fact is that with gestures of kindness, activities, and some extra effort, you can actually boost the level of performance of everyone on your team, minimizing the critical nature of the naysayers and perhaps supercharging the peak performers. Some things are easy, like being sure to talk about yourselves as a team, using words like "we" and "us" and "nobody does it better." It is an attitude that will spread to everyone.

Following are a few simple ideas and tenets of schmoozing your employees and co-workers. They may sound obvious, even simple, but think for a moment about your office and when the last time was that you actually did really positive group things like them.

- Treat your employees and co-workers more like family, not a number.

- Encourage and participate in company outings such as picnics, boat trips, road rallies, or ball games.

- Invite others' families to company outings, and show a genuine interest in them.

- Dress up for Halloween on the job for the customers.

- Wear Santa hats during the holidays, and lead customers in caroling.

- Have a birthday party hit squad make up their very own unique arrangement of the standard happy birthday song, complete with drums, tambourine, maracas, and a funny ending.

- Make sure you have your own special holiday party.

- Book entertainment such as a comic or magician for your office parties.

- Whenever possible, hold these special events during working hours.

With a little work and a lot of schmooze, you can create a group that looks forward to seeing each other every morning and working together as a team. They have a strong leader who is committed to seeing the team excel. As individuals, they soothe and schmooze each other. They've been given special training to assure group cohesiveness, such as conflict management, communication styles, change management, or sexual harassment seminars. They may even go on non-work related outings together to play and socialize. And they probably have a system set up for airing grievances, discussing disagreements, and venting pent-up frustrations.

Finally, remember that schmoozing is a circular activity. When your employees begin to schmooze, they will enjoy their jobs more and perform them better. Once they see the positive results it brings, they will take their schmoozing ability back to their home lives, ideally making their spouses and children happier. A happier home life should in turn make for an even happier employee at work and, not surprisingly, a better schmoozer. So you see, the circle is complete and constantly rotating in a positive direction.

As the boss, try to create a workplace like no one else's. Things will happen to your people, like losing a spouse, encountering a family illness, or dealing with a troubled teen at home. By showing that you have a caring and supportive attitude, you will see higher productivity and lower turnover.

CHAPTER NINE

THE SCHMOOZING NINJA SALESPERSON

Profit by Your Endearment

Nobody has ever bought anything from a company. They have only bought things from a person.

I choose to think the two words "sales" and "schmoozing" are the same word. If you are a salesperson, I truly believe that this chapter is only one small part, because this whole book is what sales is all about—schmoozing and selling yourself.

I'd like to start this chapter with a story I've been told is true. I know the three greatest ninja salespeople, Bud Frankel, from Frankel and Company, Allan Brown, with Simon Marketing, and Tom Feeney, from Group II. They told me this story about a huge discount chain (you know the one I'm talking about, they have the happy senior citizens schmoozing you right at the door). Now, when entering the front door of their national headquarters' office, there are actual church pews situated in front of a huge round information desk. You tell the lady behind the desk who you want to see and then take a seat in the church pews. Sooner or later, you will be called back to the desk and instructed to go down a long hall. On each side of the hall are little sliding glass cubical doors, which salespeople refer to as "sweat boxes." With whatever you are trying to sell this huge chain, you will be coming back down that hall a chump or a champ, because they don't buy just one of what you have, they will buy many, and if you make a sale here today, you've done well, champ!

The story goes that the salesperson had nice little fans...desk fans. He told the buyer, "my absolute bottom price is $19."

"I can't buy those at $19. I can buy them at $16.50," the buyer said.

"There's no way. I am making nothing at $19. It is my very bottom price," replied the salesperson.

"$16.50 is all we can go," said the buyer.

"You really have to come up to $19," the seller said.

"Today, you will sell no fans at $19," the buyer replied, "but you can sell 250,000 fans at $16.50."

"Okay, $16.25 it is."

It's December, and the other day, I was working the handicapped Christmas show for the Showman's League Association at the Medinah Temple in Chicago. It was early in the morning on a windy, sub-zero temperature day. I was in my van, I was warm, and I was lost. There was a guy selling newspapers on the corner, so I stopped to ask him for directions. He gave them to me, wished me a happy holiday, and reminded me, "Ain't it a great day to be alive?" He made my day with that statement. I was warm, and he was freezing. "Ain't it a great day?" It instantly reminded me that I needed a paper. He so endeared himself to me that I had to have one of those $5 papers. I heard later that both the TV and news media in Chicago had done stories on this guy and his ever-positive attitude and wonderful power of making people feel good about themselves. Was he schmoozing me? I hope so!

I said that sales and schmoozing are synonymous. Let me give you another pair of synonyms—"Schmoozing" and "endearment." I recently returned from a business trip in Mexico. While I was there, I visited one small marketplace that stands out in my mind. There was a standard hawking of wares in the market; basically a loud-voiced thrusting of products in your face. It was the kind of market that almost immediately makes you reach the point where even if there is something you want to buy, there's just too much pressure to buy it. You'll take a pass on purchasing it because the experience itself is just too annoying.

There is a lesson to be learned here. In this same place, I passed a gentlemen whose English was fairly good, but his sense of humor was even better. He was selling something I thought I didn't even want—serape— you know, those rug-looking things with a hole through the top. As I passed him, he said, "You would look great in one of these. They cost almost nothing. As a matter of fact, we're giving them away—but we make it up in volume! Never mind, pay me the next time you see me!"

Of course, I would never see him again, which made his last comment hilarious. He had me laughing so hard I turned around and said, "what are you selling?" Well, I can tell you what he was selling because it's hanging over the chair I'm sitting in as I write this. Once he caught my interest, he had time to explain the many uses of his poncho (a picnic blanket, for warmth if it gets cold suddenly, for carrying things). He was totally endearing. Just talking to him was worth the price of something I didn't really need. What he really was selling was endearment, and I bought it—lock, stock, and serape.

When I was eighteen, I quickly learned that this endearment quality was the key to sales. I had taken a job as a used car salesperson. Though the cars were less than a deal, I quickly became the top-selling salesperson. At sales meetings, we were told how bad some of the cars (lemons) were, and though I felt guilty for pawning these heaps off on the unwitting public, I also knew that I needed the money. At that young age, I would willingly swap my integrity for a paycheck.

I quit that job for two reasons. First, I didn't believe in what I was doing and felt pretty bad about some of the cars I sold, and second, it was too easy. Having grown up working in the carnival, I know it's easy to cheat and scam. It's more of a challenge to do whatever you do honestly. As the saying we had in the carnival goes, "it's easy to cheat 'em, it's harder to beat 'em."

As my father told me, "believe in what you sell, and sell what you believe in." In the same vein, he also said, "when you like doing something, go do it, and then figure out a way to pay for it." So, if you're stuck selling Brand X and your competitor is selling Brand A (the better product), and you don't believe in your product, rather than trade in your integrity, get out of that job and see if you can get in with the A team. The absolute worst thing you can do is sell something you don't believe in. How often on a television news magazine do you see salespeople saying in the end how bad they felt about the people they were duping into buying their product?

But, my mother had a wonderful saying, "you don't hurt young, you hurt old." I can relate to that. I feel bad for that eighteen-year-old man who was dropping lemons on people just to get a commission, but at least I had the good sense to get away from it. Sooner or later, what goes around, comes around.

Now here's the one statement that will help you get in with the A team—if you can sell junk, you can also sell gold. The truth is that every time you're out there selling, you're putting your personality on the line. You're truly selling you. Don't you think then that the product should be as good as you?

In reality, it's a nice feeling knowing you've sold a product or service that was worth every bit of the price. That feeling alone will justify your profit. Let me give you an example of this. I once sold, literally, a carload of eyeglass polish, a bottle at a time—and I'm talking about a *railroad* car! Although it was one of those high profit items, I'll tell you, I truly believed in what that product did. Quite simply, it kept your glasses from steaming up in the winter when you went to your car. The whole package cost about $1.75, but in retrospect, would I pay $1.75 not to have my eyeglasses fog up night after night? The answer is an emphatic yes, I would! It also worked on your car windows, ovens, and your bathroom mirror. I felt in my heart that the whole thing was the best bargain in the world. Even though I was making a gob of money (I'm embarrassed to tell you the actual cost of the polish), I could honestly say this was a good product.

Years ago, I was in a comedy team called Shaye and Jaye. We were actually working in the cheesehead, Borscht Belt in southeastern Wisconsin. Yes, there actually was one—where else would the Chicago flatlanders have gone for entertainment? We would have to fight to keep our jobs and keep other comics from honing in on our gigs. Finally, two comics, Sonny Mars and Stu Allen, started a club called the Three Sheeters for all of the midwestern entertainers. Immediately, the backstabbing went away, and we were actually giving jobs to one another if we couldn't take them ourselves. There is a lesson to be learned here from these merchants of mirth—there can be camaraderie in competition. That's how mergers happen.

Believing in what you're selling and selling yourself is what this chapter is all about. For me to spend time telling you *how* to sell would be mundane. You've probably heard a hundred sales gurus and ten-step sales programs already. My program is one-step: Schmooze. In fact, I'm probably telling you something you already know about yourself but really never defined, that schmoozing is endearing and schmoozing is sales by endearment. Everything you need to know lies in every single chapter of this book. (Another great book for salespeople is *Let Me Hear Your Body Talk*, by Jan Hargrave.) No matter how great your product is, if you're not endearing yourself to that buyer so he or she will see you both as a partner and a friend, you are leaving the door open for another salesperson to take your sale.

CHAPTER TEN

THE MATCHMAKING SCHMOOZE

The Love and Business Connection

There are two kinds of matchmaking: the first is the networking of putting people together for jobs or opportunities, and the second is putting people together because you're a romantic and you think they'll look cute together. Yeah, you guessed it: I am the male version of Dolly Levi from "Hello, Dolly." But what I'm doing when I'm playing matchmaker is gathering an army of people who I know I can depend on. I'm enlarging my support group.

Don't be afraid to get involved in a positive way in other people's lives. A small word of caution here: always make sure you are doing it for the benefit of the other people, not for your own benefit. Do it to help people get a job, or put them together with the right person to get a job, or do it just to make new friends. But before you do so, make sure they can cut it, because they are going in on your recommendation. So know your people. And in the end, that's what's fun about this—you get to know people better.

The great game of matchmaking is to help some friends venture through the maze of meeting their mate. I call it a maze because that's what it exactly is. We enter the maze in our teens making a lot of bad love choices and sometimes (God forbid) a lifetime mistake. Literally throwing pearls to swine, this age is the most dangerous part of the maze. What we are doing here is learning how to turn when we hit the wall. If you fight the maze, you lose—you must learn to turn. You may hit a wall that might make you think you've found your mate, but upon closer examination of the behavior of this wall, even through the camouflage and the flowery wallpaper, you somehow make the right decision and turn. You now get to go on, sadder but wiser because now you have gathered some clues of what and who you're really looking for. Your reward at the end of the maze is your mate, waiting for you with a couple of carats or a big kiss. I suggest that if you're a parent of teens, let them read this paragraph. Some will give you a look like a pig looking at a wristwatch and say "So..." while others will get it and know being forewarned is being forearmed.

I have introduced twelve couples who have since married, and out of the twelve, only one is angry with me. There are several ways to do this kind of matchmaking. You can start by telling one part of the future couple that you're going to do a fix-up. Generally, I just tell the girl, "girlfriend, do I know somebody you may like to go out with!" If she's willing, I tell her, "I'll give him your phone number (I suggest that we give him a work number, that way he doesn't have the home number in case this doesn't work out)."

My most recent success was a classy lady who had been alone far too long after the death of her husband. I realized she would have to have a pretty classy guy in order for a match here. My buddy Dominick works at a high fashion clothing store on Michigan Avenue in Chicago. So I told him, "I know a classy lady who's not meeting the right kind of men in her league, Dom, do you know any gentlemen customers who are single, widowed or divorced, and need a shot at meeting a great lady?" Sure enough, right off the top of his head he knew somebody. Today, these two people are happily married, and Dom was thrilled to be part of it. See how easy it can be?

Before you try any matchmaking, you should at least know a little about each party, because if this thing turns out bad, you don't want to lose a friend. The best advice here is to confront both "fix-up-ees" and tell them that if it starts not to feel right, you must break clean so all parties can still talk and be friends the next day. Do your homework. Find out if anybody is boomeranging. Let them know it's crass to hit on anybody on your first date. If one of them just had a bad break-up, don't let them bring dirty laundry or old baggage with them. OK, so you sound like their mother here. Try to remember that your friendship is hanging in the balance. Any way it plays out, you will either be the benefactor or the terminator.

Overall, I'm a hopeless romantic. Anytime I see a man or woman who is alone or shy or overworked, or married to a job and simply going home at night to watch the VCR, I feel it is my duty to find another person doing the exact same thing and put them together.

If you're going to get into this matchmaking game, here are some angles you can try. Putting two people together is tricky business. First, guys are blind, speechless, and hearing and thinking impaired. You almost have to hit them over the head to let them know a girl's coming on to them. Yeah, men can be really stupid. For example, I was working in a comedy club with a friend of mine named Mark Shilobrit. A beautiful waitress at the club had been giving him all sorts of face and body language that she was interested in him. It was obvious to me, though, that he wasn't picking up.

Moments later, we were in the green room (the comics' hangout in clubs), I said, "are you not picking up on that waitress because you're already going out with someone?" He said, "What are you talking about, she isn't into me."

"Dummy, watch this...Being an older guy you can do this," I told him with a wink. I called her over and asked her if she liked Mark. She shyly put her head down and said yes. "He's asked me to ask you to go out with him." Once again, she said yes. At which time, Mark took over like the Marines landing in Saudi and said, "Yeah, I had to have Aye Jaye ask you because I was too shy; how about tonight?" Yeah, right!

Matchmaking works best when you have a partner in crime—for me it's often my wife. When we get in cahoots to do some matchmaking, she generally invites the girl, and I'll invite the guy. Because there are always so many things you can do only as couples, we play participation sports where they'll have to be a team together, like a road rally, where they're alone in the same car, or a bocci ball game, where they'll be partners. Then, let nature take it's course.

Often during conversation, people tell me they wish they could find a companion. I tell them the best place is the workplace. You've got customers, suppliers, and a constant flow of new workmates, coming and going. Or you could put yourself where the action is. Do you scuba-dive? Take a trip, you'll meet someone. If you're into planes, horses, bottle cap collecting, you'll find your mate here, or take a single's cruise or go to the Boscabel or Negril (Jamaica) or any hot singles places in the Caribbean. And don't count out weddings or funerals as good places to meet people. The number one key is to not just hide out at home, and don't forget to keep your eye open during the work day! Keep in mind, again, that sexual harassment is in the eye of the beholder and that you need to be especially cautious.

I also match up people with situations. If I know a booker with good comics and I also know of a club that has a stage but no entertainment and no business to match—and I think it would be a beneficial arrangement—I get them together. Or I may know a good carpenter that I recommend to a friend who needs some work done. I do it if I know the carpenter's doing a job really well and my friend will pay her more for the same job, just for the expertise, even if it means losing her myself. It's bad luck to hold anybody back.

I have a reputation of being able to get it better, get more of it, get it quicker, and get it cheaper than anybody else. The reason I am able to do that is because I collect people. I know where different talents are—Eric Clark and Dick Steinberg are the best lawyers, Mike Wichger's a great chiropractor, Georgia Rapkin is the best acupuncturist, Dennis Iglar and Dale Johnson are the best doctors, Brian Bergman's the best dentist, Pat Johnson, with a machine shop in the garage, does the best car work in the world, and Don Miller is the best barber.

If I buy what you're selling and I like it and I know other people who can use it, I'm going to turn them onto you. I've done it with things as small as personalized paper clips, all the way up to merging large companies.

You see, matchmaking isn't just about couples and romance, it's about people. Specifically, it's about you going out of your way to make other people happy. And remember, your matchmaking gesture can be as large or small as fits the situation. The person you found that obscure old album for may be just as appreciative as the one for whom you found a spouse. Either way, you've added something great to their life!

Try to remember that single people are always in lust before they are in love—that's why they always have the greatest underwear.

CHAPTER ELEVEN

SCHMOOZING FOR LOVE

Love Is Grand, Divorce Is Well over Twenty Grand

G uys, if you're in the shopping market hunting for babes and you see two good-looking gals in the produce department and they have rings on their fingers—forget about it. Gals, if you're in the produce department and you see two good-looking guys and they have sweaters tied around their necks—forget about it.

This is my favorite chapter, my absolute favorite one, yet this the most difficult and complex of all of them. I know a lot about this subject because I married very late. I was in my late thirties when I married my first wife, Annie, who rocks my world. I love marriage, but I miss sex (just kidding Annie).

Now I've dated a lot of women and know a lot about the subject, but please don't judge me, because I loved every one of them. Women are my favorite human beings. I love their femininity, their style, their endurance, their strength—they walk before us, they talk before us, they potty train before us, they live longer, they're not in our jails, they take pain better, most of them are more trustworthy, they own all the insurance, they are constantly evolving, they don't lose their hair, and in child-birth alone they share creation with God. I love the smell of them, being around them, and listening to them—they have a giggle in their talk and a wiggle in their walk and they make the world go 'round. (Can I get an AMEN?!) So you can imagine I thanked the Good Lord when she granted me two daughters.

I know what you're thinking. What makes me qualified to even dare pontificate on this subject? Well, here are my qualifications: I've had my ups and downs, I've won and lost, I've either driven or someone drove me crazy. I fell down seven times and got up eight. At this point in my life, I'm even thankful for the relationships that were horrible, and it is certainly said that it is better to have loved and lost, than never to have loved at all. Trite, but true.

Finding Your Partner

What camouflage appears when two people meet and like one another? At this early point in a relationship, everybody's on their best behavior in every respect, from your appearance to your manners to keeping your apartment clean and licking your teeth to check for crud between them.

Now this camouflage is very tricky, because everybody is being so good and you are inhaling such large whiffs of ambrosia that the brain doesn't quite work right. I remember one such incident early on in my bachelorhood when I was so infatuated with a Ferrari girl (you know the type, big hair, lips, teeth, eyes, all the better to be seen with) that I remember thinking that I just *had* to spend the rest of my life with her. And I also remember thinking three weeks later, "Oh my God, how can I fake my death?" My father said "behind every drop-dead, good-looking guy or girl is someone they're a pain in the ass to."

I've lived through a great time, where the world changed rapidly and gender roles changed with it. These years have brought new definitions of what it means to be a man and also the advent of women's liberation (but my mother said she liked it the way it was when women were *superior*, not equal).

It is a whole new game now, because women will take the initiative to make the first advance. But, you have to start by getting out into the ballgame in the first place. If you want to find that special someone, you're certainly not going to do it sitting at home, talking about it, feeling bad about it, or just plain not doing anything about it. "I've tried it, and it didn't work," you say? Well quit complaining and try again. Be more creative this time. And although bars, churches, and the produce section of the grocery store may be the most obvious, they are not necessarily the best places to look.

The first thing to consider when going out to seek a romantic match is your own interests. Somewhere within your own interests is a partner that you already have something in common with. Take anything inside your head that you like to do—make a list if you have to. Whether it is a hobby, an activity, or a sport, whatever you like, people you'll like will be at these same places, and you've just increased your odds for romance. For example, community theater gives a lot of people an opportunity to meet somebody with similar interests. Volunteer groups, dance workshops, weddings, and even funerals are all places that people can meet. Don't laugh at my suggestion of funerals. My buddy Kate Launder, in her late thirties, went to a neighbor's funeral and met the long-lost son, a Sean Connery look-alike from California. Three weeks later, on one knee, he put a rock on her finger the size of Michigan's upper peninsula. And yes, he even asked her father for her hand (after her father got done kissing his hand).

Here's another example: if you love Chinese food, take a Chinese cooking course at a local college. This example actually worked for a friend of mine—it's how he met the woman he married. At the end of every class, Bill and Suzanne got to eat whatever they cooked that evening. For eight weeks, they ate the best Chinese food that ever cost only $2.50 a plate, and they're still cooking for one another today—every once in a while they make Chinese food too! As another example, Tommy and Tammy joined a local college massage course where they gave an hour of massage and received an hour of massage. They joined separately, but graduated together. Incidentally, they are still massaging.

My mother, Matka, had a wise saying: "Every pot has a cover." So, let's get a lid on this thing, and if you're not cracked, you'll find your cover.

LOVE 'EM OR LEAVE 'EM?

So now you've found someone, and you need to decide whether you want to keep him or her. This is a time for some serious soul searching. If you've lost before at this game of love, then you're definitely sadder but wiser, but again, in the words of my mother, "What vas, vas."

As an important part of your soul searching, think about what went wrong in your last relationship. If you've made it past the first and second dates and there is going to be a third, something is happening here. Once it starts to happen, it's wonderful. Everybody's on their best behavior—but hold that thought. Are you on your best behavior because you're hiding something? Or does your best behavior just naturally hide some ugly habits? Do your relationships usually go along fine until you feel comfortable enough to drop your shields and show the true Mister or Mistress Hyde you really are?

If you are hiding something—intentionally or unintentionally—and that's what jinxed up your last relationship, it's time to put that in check and fix it. If you're really thinking this could be a relationship that lasts, drop those shields now. How you and your partner work through it will show you a lot about the true depth of your relationship.

Now here's a novel question to ask during your soul searching of what went wrong in your last relationship: were you too cheap? Are you cheap with your money and your time? To you, all I can say is spend, spend, spend. A relationship is a big investment, and there's nothing in the world more interesting than another single person. You are looking for someone to be with, aren't you?

The truth is that relationships can be a great investment. There can be no finer money and time spent than on this person. To whatever the limits of your spending can be, spend it and keep on spending it, because you're spending it on yourself and a person you want to be with. You're also making things good for each other, which will make things good for yourself. To think more about the other person than you do about yourself is the key, and more about "us" than "me." For example, on my third date with my wife, I gave her a gold bracelet with my phone number inscribed on the inside.

Anybody who has been in love realizes (especially the second time around) that it was they themselves that let love down. It is wonderful to be in love and infatuated, talking on the phone for hours, holding hands, touching, opening doors, being mannerly, affectionate, constantly clever, polite, and considerate. But perhaps then it was so nice that you took things for granted and it was at least partly your fault that the relationship died. You realize that the next time those fields of ambrosia come your way, you will hang on to them longer.

Okay, let's move forward. Let's say that you finally have a date, and you've passed each other's physical requirements. I will still stick to "pretty is as pretty does," because the dripping beauties I've dated who took two and a half hours to get ready, in the end, didn't really seem worth it. I work with a lot of young people, and I see one common mistake being made over and over—they make their moves too quickly, and if they're the same age, the guy tends to take the girl for granted. This is where slow savoir faire will pay off on both the girl's or the boy's part. Remember, slow and steady wins the race.

Anyway, after a great two-week, polite romance, one of the two partners in your relationship should make the move to say that it has been a wonderful two weeks and suggest a renewal of the same thing for two more weeks with an option for an additional two weeks after that. Now use some inventiveness to keep it hot and moving forward. Find things to do other than just going to the movies. And remember, not just one, but both partners should be coming back to the relationship with new adventures such as camping trips, river rafting, skiing, festivals that are taking place in your area, and any other great activities and adventures. Surprise each other (and surprise yourself) with your inventiveness.

A perfect example is my friend Dave Batt, the wine guru, who collected forty bottles of the best vintage wine dating back forty years for his girl-friend Alex's fortieth birthday present. He presented them to her on her birthday, but kept them at his house. Good schmooze Dave!

Okay, now you've gotten through the ambrosia. You've prolonged it as long as you can, and you are officially "an item." You're even thinking about cohabiting. Though I do not believe that there's an eleventh commandment that says, "Thou shalt not have fun alone," spending even more time with this person sounds like tremendous fun. And you're looking for a healthy, mature, productive situation, where each person is allowed to grow as an individual and perform as a team, experiencing the full rich adventure of life together. Beware of your biggest enemy, silence.

Our first kiss or consummation is usually in silence. We don't talk about how we like to be kissed or made love to, we just do it. The first time we make love, the moment is right for both of us. We don't ask for it, we just do it, usually in silence. And the silence goes on from there. Now when we're angry with one another, we punish with silence. During long periods of anger, we sleep silently, and back-to-back (which can only be enjoyable when done with another couple—just kidding).

So this time around you have to be on an amazing search for that one human being who can act as a reactor for your love. All you need to obtain it is the opposite of silence, talking it out in front. Bargain for it, plead for it, but get it, or don't go on, because your alternative is becoming one of the multitude of slugs on the highway of mediocrity. Your role models and mascots here should be swans—they mate for life.

If it looks like this relationship is going to be in for a long run, you've learned from your past mistakes, and most importantly, before you jump in any further than you are ready, get ready to talk it out and keep on talking it out. Let each other know what you like and dislike and especially how you would like to be treated, and then agree to indulge the other person. Talking it out is the only way to get it out in front on every issue. If you think you're going to marry, dive in up to your follicles with total commitment. What do you have to lose? If you're planning on getting married, then tell each other that you're in it for the long haul. Woo each other and support each other for life.

At this serious point in the relationship, stop, step back, and check out your inner motives. Why do you want to take a partner? Loving another person is not a good enough reason, because you can love anything—your dog, cat, car, etc....but you can't be in love with these things. So re-examine your rationale here. Your goal should be looking for a lifetime nirvana on earth with your mate. That means not just to love them but to set your goals to be in love with them until one of you goes on ahead to build that big condo in the hereafter. That love you had in your lifetime supplies the building materials for that three-level condo, complete with a riding vacuum cleaner, in the hereafter.

Finally, if you do decide to marry this person, get in a car and drive from one coast to the other. In the next long hours, the Gaston or Cruella in you will show their ugly heads. Oh, and I'm as serious as a heart attack here—I once drove from Wisconsin to Florida in a new relationship in a Buick, and I came home on a Boeing. Now you might think me a cad to have deserted her, but my other choice was to spend the rest of my life in a small room with a guy named Bubba who wanted me to tattoo his name on my arm. You can turn around and come right back. If you can still even talk to one another when you get home, marry that person immediately. If not, you've just equaled seven years of marriage in the confines of that car. Don't try and shove it if it doesn't fit.

Men and Women under One Roof

Obtaining an equal fairness must be the ultimate goal in your relationship. It is the key to succeeding in a relationship where you have committed to sharing your everyday lives together. A fair relationship is equal parts love, honesty, respect, and effort. But we men often misinterpret the idea of "fair." To us, it's only fair that we get to keep a separate part of our life that hangs onto pieces of youth and bachelorhood that don't include our mate. That old crony thing—those nights out with the boys, being a member of three baseball teams, or making her a TV or sports widow—is probably the number one reason for losing that whole wonderful thing you had going. Then when another guy comes along and sympathizes with her, you can't figure out why you got dumped.

You should be looking for a best friend that you can make love to. You should not be looking for a housekeeper or financier, meaning you need an equal opportunity kitchen as well as house. Without being overly stereotypical, again, men are the fault here mostly because of moms who spoiled them by cooking and washing for them. Many come to expect it. They should, in fact, be doing a 180 degree turnaround to show how self-sufficient and caring they can be. These are the exact skills being taught to men who are trying to save their marriages, and they are generally the biggest assets that help them save it.

One of my dearest friends had no idea how much he loved his wife until she moved out of the house and informed him she was filing for divorce. He proposed a plea bargain for a three-month extension before she filed, to better himself to get back their marriage. He then enrolled in a costly, male-oriented marriage counseling course. Well it worked. As I write, they are expecting a child. Today, when he looks back at his old self, he still can't believe how he ever became such a controlling pig and how she took it for so long. He no longer sees her as a housewife, but as his loving icon mate. *Webster's Dictionary* defines icon as: "a person or thing that is revered or idolized."

For the women reading this, we men are generally blind to this and need all the help we can get. So try as pleasantly as you can to confront, confront, confront. We react to sweet tones better than anything else, so keep at us, but keep it sweet, and you'll find you can start to straighten out some of those bad habits.

Before cohabitation starts, the two of you should have a lengthy talk, making a list of each of your duties and what life will be like. You are about to get a good display of who each of you really is. I've often thought that the honeymoon doesn't really come after marriage, but lasts from your very first meeting up until the time you are married. Then things take a little more work. They say there is a food that if ingested by couples will ruin their sex lives. It's called wedding cake. But it doesn't have to be that way. I once heard a female comedienne say that the honeymoon is over when the "passing gas" stage of their relationship starts or in the morning when he's standing at the sink shaving and she's sitting on the toilet. Being comfortable with one another is a wonderful thing. Just remember that you're trying to marry your soulmate, and you're hoping by some act of faith that you've actually found that person. You're praying that your true life mate isn't cooking a falafel over a dung fire in some third world country. So talk it out at every step of the way, keep working at it, don't just act on your best behavior, *become* your best behavior.

MARRIAGE—SCHMOOZING FOR LIFE

The only thing I take seriously in my life is my wife, Annie Jaye. If I could get two weeks off, I'd want to spend them with her. I don't love my wife, I'm in love with my wife. Anyone can love, it's harder to be in love. That's what takes some work. We realized from the start that each one of us would be each other's prime objective. In our wedding vows (which was as normal as a marriage can be with an elephant for a ring bearer), we proclaimed that once a week, every week, we would have a "date night." Even today we do it, and it has kept our marriage continually surprising and exciting.

Date night is a simple concept: all you have to do is commit one night a week only to each other. It doesn't matter what day of the week it is (although a semi-regular schedule may make it easier, especially if you have kids), and it doesn't matter who initiates it—no one's keeping score. But the one who initiates it has to handle planning the whole thing from start to finish (even the baby-sitter). The other person has no clue where they're going or what they're doing. They are simply told what time to be ready and what to wear. The excitement begins right when you pull out of the driveway. At that point, whether we turn east or west will tell us if we're going uptown or downtown. It can be anything from a simple trip to the movies to a day trip to New York City to have lunch at Tavern on the Green and see a Broadway play. Sometimes we even include the kids, especially when it's most appropriate, like last week when we went to the circus parade with a packed lunch and a blanket.

The rules of our relationship always stay in order. They were printed a long time ago. Nobody goes to bed with *mad* on or you can't get *anything else* on. We don't seem to have many arguments, because if we do, we use courtesies like, "forgive me, but I need to vent," or "forgive me, but I'm passionate about this one," or "this one's important to me, let's talk." Even if we disagree, it's hardly an argument when you're being so honest and so darn polite. And we learned long ago not to sweat the Ulysses— we only fight Cyclops. We're pretty fussy about what we raise our dander over.

Guys, whether you're still in search of the right person or just trying to work it out with the current one, try to remember that there's a brand new "2000

Woman" out there. She's in the workplace, she's three-dimensional, and she's constantly evolving. She's no longer looking for the hunter/gatherer—she often makes more money than you. She's looking for a strong partner in a relationship that will contain integrity, trust, honor, sharing, and caring. And gals, remember that men have evolved a bit too. We might be a little more thoughtful and sensitive than you think, and perhaps we're even more ready to partner with the "2000 Woman."

With all that in mind, try to think of new ideas to keep it hot and heavy, and find out where all those new pleasure buttons are to be pushed. Be creative about what new games you can play together, what the proper gifts are to give, and where to leave a love note that will be found during the day.

The greatest highs I've ever had in my life are the ether-breathing feelings of being in love (and I know high—I was told that the sixties were good to me). Before Annie and I married, we sat down one afternoon on the shores of Lake Okauchee and punched out our marriage manifesto on paper. We wanted to agree on what marriage would and should be like for us. We talked about traits we didn't like in our ex-partners, our parents, and ourselves. When we were done, we embraced and tearfully headed off into our lives together. Twelve years and two great kids later, we have honored to the letter our own marriage manifesto, and we're still here. So here's what is in ours. You may want to make up your own based around this, our baker's dozen on how to achieve being in love:

1. Always work toward perfection in your relationship and keep a healthy passion within it. When you feel things have changed, rewrite your manifesto.

2. Cheating is the biggest lie on earth, so there can be no dishonesty in your relationship. The truth will set you free.

3. Make up a safe word to get a time-out, especially if it starts to look like it's going to get loud.

4. No silent warfare. It's a silent killer.

5. Never go to bed with a mad on. It's not healthy physically or mentally.

6. Never cry over anything that can't cry over you. Nobody gets to be a material girl or boy.

7. Pledge allegiance to your mate, and to your marriage for which it stands, one last line of defense, with liberty and justice for us.

8. Always cover off your mate with what's going on inside and outside of you.

9. Have date night once a week, every week, forever.

10. Think up random acts of kindness for one another. Do it daily.

11. Do not work toward love, work toward *being in love*.

12. Agree that you are one another's precious icon, and then act accordingly.

13. Together, try to die young at an old age.

I'm always looking for new sources of ideas that will help keep the spice in a relationship and have just found one I'd like to share with you: it's called *Love—The Course They Forgot To Teach You In School*, by Gregory J.P. Godek. When I finish it, I'll get a second book to read—also by Godek—entitled, *1001 Ways To Be Romantic*.

It was Hemingway who said, "when two people love one another there can possibly be no happy ending." However, I choose to believe Andrew Lloyd Webber, who says that loving another is seeing the face of God. Through all stages of love, look for creative ways to keep the electricity alive. Remember, it is easier to maintain a relationship than it is to fix one.

CHAPTER TWELVE

MAKING UP
SCHMOOZE

I Was a Jerk, but I'm Better Now

A husband and wife had driven in silence for miles after a horrible argument. The husband finally pointed to a jackass in the pasture, "Relative of yours?" he asked. She replied, "Yes, by marriage."

Admittedly, it took a lot of relationships and testosterone-letting before I was able to figure out why I would want to tick off my corner person, backup, alibi, lover, and the last human being on earth willing to give me mouth-to-mouth. So now that you've gotten through the romantic, polite, good behavior that got you into this relationship in the first place, let me give you the schmooze fight rules laid down by the Sadder but Wiser State Aesthetics Board. (Fight Aware: will remind you that until you figure out that synchronized arguing is not a winning pairs event, you are doomed to repeat the contest. En garde!)

HOW TO FIGHT

When a fight starts, the feeling is betrayal (equal to and just as bad as when Rolf blew that whistle in *The Sound of Music*). They say that making up is hard to do, but that's only true if you're a hard-head or a meat-head. If you walked away from an argument or fight with someone you care about and discovered you were wrong about whatever happened, be quick to admit it, apologize, and snap out of it. If, indeed, that is your problem—that you always hurt the one you love—when you get done with your huff, get back to them, explain and apologize, and thank them for allowing you to vent. Reassure them that you will try not to do it again.

If you truly feel that the fight wasn't your fault and you feel it was brought on by other life pressures on the other person, try to accept it for a while. At a calmer moment, let the person know how you felt so next time they can find another whipping boy or girl.

Here's a helpful tip for keeping your relationships healthy—before your first fight in your next relationship, or *right now* in your current relationship, make rules for fighting, such as:

- No yelling—being louder doesn't mean you're right

- Don't do anything physical, either partner

- Know that what was, was

- No name calling

- No slamming things—those are kids' tricks

- Cut to the chase, and no lying

- No drama or trying to be an aspiring young actor

As an additional bonus, I recommend that you make up pleasure punishments for your rules. If either partner breaks any of the above rules, activate a pleasure punishment. They are win, win. You can make up some of your own, but here are some of mine:

- One hour foot rubs

- "Take you to dinner, I pay"

- "Take you to a movie, you pick"

- Toys for boys, pearls for girls

- Love favors (a good way to forgive and forget)

If you are working on your great relationship, there is no need to start a fight to get any of the above list. Remember, these rules should be set at the very beginning of a serious relationship—before there's a first confrontation or before you feel that foolish need to start one.

Here's another helpful hint: To avoid feelings getting hurt the next time around (and hopefully there won't be one), arrange for a safe word that will signal to your partner that you or your partner needs to vent. A good phrase to use could be something like "let's reset" (just like on the back of appliances to keep them from burning up). Once your code phrase is established, any confrontation will be less threatening. It will give you both a chance to strike your "I understand" stance. You'll also have the time to make the decision to let it pass when it isn't a big deal. Remember to talk it out from time to time, so the next time both of you need to vent, you'll have established a sort of "asking permission." This at least allows your partner to prepare for it and get braced. When you get it done, be ready to reward that partner for indulging you in that painful favor, because if you truly care for them, that's what it really is about.

Be willing to take your whacks if the cause of the argument was your fault, or explain why you have to stand your ground on this one. This method of arguing is less personal, and the tone of it seems to stay respectful. This works especially well in business where these confrontations are commonplace several times a day.

There is a quote from an old movie that goes, "Love means never having to say you're sorry." That was the worst statement I've ever heard in my life. Don't ever be afraid to say you're sorry! That kind of understanding between two people will keep your relationship strong forever.

MAKING UP

To stop a fight, go up and kiss your partner and tell them you can't fight when you're kissing—I call this "schmooze smooching." Also, after love-making is a good time to talk about bettering your relationship. It's also just a good time to talk. You can hear and think better when you've just returned from a romp through nirvana.

Start thinking of a Making Up Schmooze. If you're good partners, you'll be aware of the dark side that lives within the two of you, and you can make sure that the pleasure in your relationship always outweighs the pain by 90 percent. When the chips are down and you're backed against the wall, you'll be looking for your partner to come through for you. So, mend those fences and make up for those infractions.

If, however, the signs say you have a break up coming, and hey, you don't want to break up, here are some helpful hints that may help you save your relationship:

1. Get counseling or professional help. The fact that you have to pay someone to listen to you doesn't mean there's something wrong with you. Believe me, these people have heard worse stories than yours, and they really can help.

2. Go on a trip and talk it out. Just get away from your ordinary routine.

3. Think about what it was you liked about this person when you first met him or her. Make a list, write it down. Send it to them in a love note. Sing it to them. No matter what you think you must do, you must tell them.

4. On the other hand, think about what it was that your mate first liked about you when you met. What can you do at this point to reassemble some of that person?

5. Talk with your partner about how you have both changed since the time you met. What's for the better, and what's for the worse?

6. Think about when in your relationship you allowed talking to stop.

7. Make concessions of what you are willing to do, give, or give up to make it work again.

8. Give a peace offering.

9. Remind one another that you don't change partners, you just change problems.

10. Remember, it isn't over until Roseanne sings!

One last thing, while we're on the subject: Be downright choosy of what you are willing to argue about. One night on *The Late Late Show* with Tom Snyder, boxing champion Oscar De La Hoya was once challenged to a fight by a street tough in his old neighborhood. De La Hoya started laughing and wisely answered, "my amigo, I don't fight for nothing." So let the little ones go (David), and only fight the "giants" (Goliath). Let's say you're convinced the cause of the dispute is not your fault, but the issue doesn't amount to a hill of garbonzos. It's not a biggy. Bite the bullet on those, and above all, try to see the other person's point of view. The only side effects are better days, months, and years in your relationship.

Now, watch out for conflicts over what is a "David" and what is a "Goliath." If you feel this one is a major issue and he or she thinks it's not worth the trouble, keep at him or her. Rome wasn't built in a day, and if your partner has any conscience at all, they'll come around when they finally realize that your motives are pure and you're only trying to achieve mutual respect for each other.

Lastly, make a Fight Aware rule early in your relationship that, because the two of you are above the average herd, you will rewrite your relationship whenever needed, always working toward perfection. And I'm here to tell you, yes, you can put fighting behind you. You can get over it.

CHAPTER THIRTEEN

THE IMPULSE IMPROV

A Lifesaving Schmooze

O f all the chapters in this book, Impulse Improv is the most note-worthy. It's about schmoozing when your life depends upon it. And nothing is as important as your life! Impulse Improv is about spinning a story web to catch a dangerous opponent off-guard. It's about acting as though you believed your own schmooze. It's the ultimate "use it" or "lose it" schmooze, as you will see.

THE STAKEOUT

One of my better Impulse Improv's happened when I was nineteen years old. My stepfather, Arney, and stepbrother, Kurt, set up our carnival near a housing project in one of the toughest neighborhoods imaginable. One day I got midway fever, which is cabin fever in reverse. I wanted to go downtown, since it was Monday and the carnival was "dark," which meant it was closed for the day and setup was over. As I left the lot and walked down the block to catch a bus, I noticed a street gang rapidly heading in my direction. By the hungry looks on their faces, I knew I was their lunch.

After they had surrounded me, their spokesman said, "You got something for us?" Without making eye contact, I put my left wrist up to my mouth and said, "Never mind, they're just kids." Then I put my hand down to my side and said, "Beat it! This is a f____n stake-out, move the f___ out!!"

The moment I said it, the gang nervously glanced around, looking in all directions, and then split—they bought it! I took several deep breaths to calm myself because my heart was racing. I couldn't believe that my nothing-to-lose schmooze worked. From that moment on, I knew Impulse Improv would forever be a part of my life. When the gang was out of sight, I ran back to the carnival lot to change my pants, and I never ventured out again. I had put myself in the part, and for that brief moment, I thought and felt like a cop. I used this talent several other times, playing the role of a blind, mentally challenged, or deaf person. It almost became addictive—I would look for scenarios just for the chance to play another part.

High-Pressure Gun Sales

When my comedy partner Marty Shaye was drafted into the Army (I had already served my time), I began doing a single stand-up comedy act. Until that time, my partner and I had worked steadily doing the Wisconsin Borscht Belt. It's not as easy to perform solo, particularly in tough clubs. One club was so tough that they searched you to see if you were packing a gun. If you weren't, they gave you one. To get into this club, you had to go down two steps—one physically and one socially. The bartender was a hairy-knuckle type, with one long eyebrow and a brother named Cyclops. But, it was a paying gig, and I had to eat.

My job was to do five minutes of material between the show girl acts. Yes, it was a strip joint. After the fifth dancer, I had a half-hour slot to do my comedy stand-up act, making the gig worth it. During the middle of the evening, a young heckler started shouting out one-liners at me, trying to throw off my timing. He didn't know that for every high school one-liner he had, I had fifty comebacks, so I was gently baiting and bleeding him just to pass the time.

The young man continued to heckle me throughout the evening, and by the time I was to do my half-hour set, he had worked himself into a frenzy. Because I worked with my microphone in my right hand and my left hand in my pocket, he kept yelling, "What do you have in your pocket?" I ignored him at first, but then he did it again—this time, right on top of one of my punch lines. I looked down at him and said, "You're lunch!" which got a great laugh and a round of applause. People hate hecklers.

The kid turned beet red from embarrassment, which slowly turned to anger. When I finished my set, I had to walk past him to get to the back room. When I passed, he said, "I'm going to kill you, but you're going to have to apologize first." I replied, "Get out of my face. If you're not here to laugh, then leave."

Well, the heckler left, but only for a few minutes. Soon, he was back in his seat, grinning at me during my next five minute set. If I close my eyes, I can still see that fiendish grin of his.

After this short set, he motioned to me as if to say, "Come on over. Let's talk. I'll buy you a drink." OK, I thought, it will be easier to work this joint if I made a friend out of this guy. A week earlier in this club, a heckler had thrown a heavy glass ashtray at a comedienne, hitting her in the face. So, talking to him seemed like a good move on my part.

When I sat on the bar stool next to him, he shoved a gun (an old Army .45) into my ribs. "I'm going to kill you anyway," he said, "but I want you to apologize first. I've just had a nice visit with a bartender in a bar down the block. I forced him onto his knees to pray in front of me." "Oh God," I thought to myself, "there's toys in this kid's attic."

There was no way I was going to slap the gun out of the hand of this maniac—it was evident this kid wasn't playing with a full deck. The first thing I felt was fear. The second was disbelief. Where were the bartenders and bouncers? Of course, they were talking and drinking at the other end of the bar. Couldn't they see in the giant mirrors behind me that this guy had a gun to my ribs and I needed help? If there was ever a time for an Impulse Improv, this was it. I figured that I'd better start talking if I wanted to escape with only a flesh wound. I thought to myself, "what character could I play this time to get myself out of this fix?"

"Time out," I said to the kid. "I'm going to apologize, but let me tell you what went down since you left. The guys sitting at the end of the bar—they're the bosses—the big one, Jimmy, just fired me for lipping back at you. I've got a wife and a set of twins (I wasn't married and didn't have kids at the time). This is my first job. I need to keep it badly, and I don't think they're going to pay me for tonight."

The heckler just sat there grinning, I felt he got some satisfaction from hearing that. "Now give me a break," I said. "I have to get some cash from somewhere, and I know the perfect place to rip off. I could really use a partner, and it's obvious to me that you're the type of gutsy guy that could help. I'd be willing to split the money down the middle." I asked him for his name, which he refused to give me, and then I said, "Bartender (Baby Joe), give my friend a drink. And give me a double, on the rocks. Oh, and you can forget the rocks."

I kept schmoozing him with this Impulse Improv, pretending as though nothing was wrong. I continued speaking to the kid as if he were my best friend and I had known him all my life. "So, if you don't want to do the robbery with me, that's OK," I said, "But I need a piece. How much money will you take for your gun?"

"It's worth over $200," he said. Was he kidding? The value of his gun, at that moment, was priceless. I was willing to sell my soul, or at least set up a payment plan, to get that gun out of his hands. So I asked the bartender to give me a draw. Now this should have tipped the bartender off that something bizarre was happening. First, I had worked this club for a while and had never bought a mark (customer), let alone an obnoxious heckler, a drink. And second, I'd never taken a draw before. But instead of leaning over the bar and cracking this guy with his ice mallet, the bartender gave me a slip of paper to sign and a draw for $200.

I thought I would die. Literally. I slid him the $200 and wondered what his next move would be. He put the money in his pocket, uncocked the gun, and said, "If you tell your buddies at the end of the bar or the bartenders or bouncers, they may beat me up, but chances are they won't kill me for you. You can call the cops, but eventually they'll let me go and I'll be back to shoot you when you're on stage." Smiling, he handed me the gun, uncocked. I knew he meant what he said. I cocked the gun and debated my next move. Should I kill him before he kills me because he's nuts?

But by then, the last record had finished, and I had to go up on stage and be funny for my final five minute set. When I turned to face the audience, I saw him leaving the bar. I remember having two thoughts: first, "If I can be funny now, I'm a comic," and second, "Wouldn't it be a hoot if this kid was a high-pressure gun salesman?" Although I never saw him at the club again, his presence lingered in every audience I ever played. I was never the same on stage again. I had a healthier attitude about messing with hecklers, and now, I won't even deal with them. Thankfully, today's clubs don't allow them. It was a hard lesson to learn, but fortunately an Impulse Improv Schmooze helped me to walk away.

When it's time for Impulse Improv, don't worry about your acting ability. The words will come if you trust yourself. You will put yourself in the role because of the desperateness of the situation. When the gun was shoved into my ribs, I instantly got cool. If you think you will be harmed, the smartest thing you can do is slow down and schmooze. Don't get crazy. Don't plead and whine. Instead, weave your attacker into your best story until you can schmooze yourself out of the situation.

Here's another example: An actor/buddy of mine in L.A., John Mendoza, who was starring on a sitcom at the time, did a great lifesaving schmooze. One night while he was parking his car, a man was crossing the street heading toward him. John noticed the guy was carrying a handgun, and he knew his intention was robbery. At this particular time, John was carrying a huge amount of money on him and knew he didn't want to lose it, so he swung himself into an Impulse Improv, pointed at the man, and yelled as loud as he could, "I didn't kill him, he was already dead. The voices in my head are liars. The state and parole board are liars. And you are one of them. And I *don't* have a tendency for violence with cutlery!" The robber did a 180 degree turn and started hot footing in the other direction. He had to be thinking he wanted nothing to do with this idiot and that John was crazier than he was. That's not even to mention the brilliance of all the noise John made while hollering his Impulse Improv.

Another improv winner is my friend John Steiner. It was a January winter in Wisconsin, and John was kissing his girlfriend goodnight in his car when a knock came on the driver's side window of the car. When he turned his head, he was looking into the business end of a revolver held by a young robber. He rolled down his window and took control. He told the kid, "Be cool, we're both in the same business. So here's my money clip and my car keys. Throw my keys in the street when you feel you're far enough away so I won't have to freeze to death in this car." The young robber did exactly as he was told, and John was happy to be out of danger and on his way. Actually, they were in the same business. Some say he *is* a robber, the way he charges his customers at his bar, Ground Zero.

When you see danger coming and it's time for an Impulse Improv, don't be afraid to start yelling to an imaginary group of friends in between some houses or calling your big dog Butkus or asking the would be robber if he's the police, because you've just been robbed and have called 911. If all is lost, throw your money to ground left and walk right.

If you've done a great acting job, who knows, maybe David Letterman or Billy Crystal will appear from thin air and hand you an Academy Award—though I haven't received one yet, despite schmoozing myself out of over five life-or-death incidents. Remember, if all else fails in a life threatening situation, THROW UP!

CHAPTER FOURTEEN

THE TRAFFIC
SCHMOOZE

How to Get Your Break Today

The last place we humans, worldwide, are willing to schmooze one another is in traffic. The minute we get in the car, it's like we've entered into a game or a showdown to beat the other contestant. You can't talk to them or hear them, so you use hand signals. You're always the smarter, better contestant in this race, so naturally, you hate the other driver. You're talking to yourself out loud in the confines of your car! You've worked yourself up into such a frenzy, you'd like to beat them like a Hitler piñata at a Hadassah picnic! The road war is on!!

STOP! Get a grip. Time to think "Road Schmooze." Let 'em in the lane. Let 'em pass. Give 'em the right of way. And then, give 'em a big wave and an OK or a thumbs up sign. Do it sincerely like you're trying to make them think you may even know them. If you do it right, they'll wave back and be embarrassed by their behavior. Now, slow, wave bye bye, and let them find someone else to play Road Roulette with. If you don't schmooze 'em, here are the only other two options: you and your passengers can lose this showdown and get hurt, crippled, or killed, or you can get a stiff ticket for the exact amount of that velvet Elvis painting you've been dying to buy.

Here's a suggestion to ease the road warrior situations you may find yourself in. Make a two-sided schmooze road sign that you can keep on your dash. On one side, put "please." On the other side, put "sorry." "Please" in a traffic jam will probably get you into a lane. "Sorry" in traffic may keep you alive in that lane. (How many times have you made a stupid driving move and apologized out loud to the other driver, even though your windows are up and you're going 55 miles an hour?) Try this for a while—you'll be amazed at how well it works.

SCHMOOZING THE COPS

If you've ever talked your way out of a speeding ticket, you're either very lucky or a good schmoozer. For those of you who complain and moan that you never get away with anything, particularly by schmoozing, this chapter may give you a few pointers so the next time you get yourself into a bind, you won't lose those precious points (or whatever system your state uses) needed for driving. I've interviewed a lot of my friends, who are also police officers, and they've given me some very interesting facts and figures about traffic tickets.

In some cities and states, cops have quotas and must set speed traps to catch speeders, so no matter what you do, if they need to fill their quota, there's no way of talking your way out of it! When an officer walks to your car window, takes your license, and without any conversation or explanation walks back to his car, he or she is probably on quota. And if it's the end of the month and he needs thirty tickets and only has twenty...will you be number twenty-one? Is Mike Tyson nervous at a spelling bee?

Be aware that if you have an out-of-state license plate, you are a prime candidate for getting a ticket, so slow down and drive the speed limit. An "over-the-border" catch is to justice as a Twinkie is to nutrition. Illinois state patrol officers refer to Wisconsin traffic offenders as cheeseheads; Wisconsin state patrol officers refer to Illinois traffic offenders as some other kind of "heads"—but I won't say what. They know that most out-of-state people will pay the fine rather than spend time and money to go to court to contest a ticket.

If you use a radar detector and you see a flashing red light behind you, grab the "fuzzbuster" and quickly throw it under the seat. Don't be stupid about it and make it look like you're trying to stash away the motherlode of drugs and weapons—you'll find yourself staring face down at the asphalt real fast. But do get that radar detector down. If you don't, you can pretty much be assured that you will receive a speeding ticket. I've interviewed at least a dozen cops who all said that once they see a fuzzbuster, in their mind, you are a speeder and that detector is a smoking gun—otherwise you wouldn't be using it.

If you are driving drunk, there's no hope for you as far as I'm concerned. You shouldn't get off. I have no schmoozes for you. You are not only risking your life, but putting other's lives in danger simply because you don't have the sense to take a cab or schmooze someone into giving you a ride home. (See how schmoozing can save lives?)

WHAT TO DO WHEN YOU GET STOPPED

When you are stopped for speeding, you have a fifty-fifty chance of getting a ticket. Let's say that you are driving in your own state, and the officer didn't see your fuzzbuster. You're a little over the speed limit, and the officer really doesn't need the quota…what should you do to turn this situation around?

If you have a good attitude and understand that the police are not "jerks" or bad guys just waiting to make your life miserable, you're halfway there. It will be helpful for you to maintain the awareness that the cops work for the average, law-abiding citizen. If you remember that 85 percent of the people the police have to deal with on a daily basis have a bad attitude, and you make an honest effort to be part of the 15 percent that are humble or humorous, they will be more likely to give you the benefit of the doubt, rather than bust you. Because most officers do have a heart, letting you go down the road with a warning rather than a ticket will make them feel good.

If you are pulled over, stop immediately, put on the emergency flashers, get your license out, and place both hands on the steering wheel with your license in your hands. The next thing you want to do is put the officer in a good mood. Let me tell you that of the cops I interviewed, all said that the first words out of your mouth are generally what gets you the ticket.

It's important to smile and greet the officer using the time of day, such as, "Good afternoon officer." If the officer asks, "Are you aware that you were going 69 miles per hour in a 55 mile per hour zone?" never admit that you know. Let me repeat that, because it's important—*never* admit that you were speeding! Don't say, "I know I was speeding but…" because once you say those words, you've just forced the officer to give you a ticket. That's their rule! If you admit to speeding, the officer must issue a ticket because you could be a spotter from the department. A "spotter" is someone who works for internal affairs whose job it is to find out if the officer is writing tickets and check his or her procedure. Also, with some police departments, certain decorum or standard operating procedures have to be exercised when approaching a car they've pulled over, as well as the manner of speaking to the driver.

At this point, the officer's expression will be serious if not scornful, since speeding is a serious matter. It's unwise to say, "What's your problem officer?" The officer doesn't have a problem…you do. And your problem is that you've just made that officer a little hotter under the collar by repeating the standard line he or she has heard a million times. So, make sure to choose your first words very carefully. Be kind, use soft tones, and smile. Of course, it wouldn't hurt to have a bumper sticker on your car that reads: Support Your Local Police Department! And then, do support them.

In many states, the officer will turn your license over to see if it's signed. What I have on the back of my license is my donor card, and what is written on one of the lines on the donor card usually catches the officer's attention. I've watched an officer squint, then start to bite his lip so he doesn't laugh, and finally give me the license back saying, "Get the hell out of here, and slow down!" The line that I've written on my donor card says, "Take genitalia, too." Ladies, this probably won't work for you, but in any case, it's a good idea to sign your donor card. It's not only a wonderful gift to someone, it also makes a positive impression on the officer.

It's always good to apologize for the transgression without admitting that you were aware of what you were doing. Say, "I'm sorry if I was speeding…I guess I wasn't paying attention." Or tell the officer why you were preoccupied, whether it is a story about something wonderful, maddening, or sad. Make sure the officer knows you have a good driving record and that you're not a speeder. Tell him or her, "I don't speed. My head may not be on straight today." They will check out your record on the computer, and if you are telling the truth, that may catch you a break and get you off with just a warning. If you've had a ticket, let them know that piece of information up front, otherwise, just keep quiet about your driving habits.

If you are driving a rental car or someone else's car, let them know that you are not familiar with that particular vehicle and maybe it just got away from you. Or, blame it on your cruise control or something mechanical with the car. If pulled over by a male officer, one friend of mine says, "Officer, I have a good excuse, but I know it's not going to be good enough for you." If the officer says, "let's hear it," my friend says, "I've been on the road, and I'm heading back home. I really have to get home soon because my wife is getting pregnant tonight, and I want to be there." If the officer laughs, he's out of there.

A friend of mine, Jerry Bouwens, told me this funny cop schmooze story just a few weeks ago. He was traveling on the freeway when he saw lights flashing in his rearview mirror. When he pulled over, the cop asked him if he knew how fast he was going. Jerry replied, "I'm going to guess over and I'm a jerk?" The cop snickered, gave him his license, and said, "Get outta here, and slow down, jerk."

Now, I personally wouldn't say these things, but after conversations with my friends, these are lines that I have heard worked:

- I was choking.

- I am sick and thought I was going to throw up.

- My head was in my butt, and I wasn't paying attention.

- I just got dumped by my boyfriend (or girlfriend) and I'm not thinking because I'm broken-hearted (who can't relate?).

- I'm very lost and was paying more attention to directions than my speed

- I need to find a bathroom, I think I have diarrhea.

- I just heard that the babysitter has not picked up my kids.

Don't think that the officers you encounter haven't heard every excuse in the book, because they have. You may just get them on a good day, and if you are polite and respectful, then you have a fighting chance of not getting that ticket. I admit that I have said to a cop, "I may have been exceeding the speed limit, but I wasn't paying attention. I'd really appreciate a break, because I don't normally speed. I'll give you my first born. I'll visit you when you're old and cover your legs with a blanket and take you for long walks in the park." I sometimes make outrageous, friendly claims, but I never get too crazy because they write down what you say.

Do you have any idea of how many different scenarios there are out on the highway of strife. Some ninety-year-old guy—who incidentally was an original cast member of the movie *Cocoon*—who has kept his driver's license has just had a major coronary, and he's coming headlong into your lane. Some stressed worker ran out of Prozac, and you just whipped him the bird. Some ying yang is delivering a trunk load of pipe bombs. Another whacko in a stolen car has an uzi laying on the front seat and a police rap sheet that reads "has a tendency for violence." Then there's the schizophrenic who sees your headlights as two motorcycles that he's going to go in between. With all these scenarios on a highway cop's plate when he's pulling you over for a simple traffic infraction, give him a break by schmoozing him so he can schmooze you back by letting you go. I've talked to cops who worked in neighborhoods you were only safe in if you were a bullet, where they're willing to let traffic violators off for just having a driver's license. So if the cop doesn't start to write, be polite.

CHAPTER FIFTEEN

THE ABC'S OF KID SCHMOOZING

If I Wrote the ABC's, I Would Be Next to U

There's an old Henny Youngman joke about a kid who doesn't talk. They take him the world over to see the best doctors, and nothing. Now the boy is six years old. One morning at breakfast, though, he looks up at his mother and says, "My French toast is burned." His mother drops to her knees in front of him and says, "You talked! You talked my son! Why haven't you ever talked before?" The kid replies, "Up 'til now, everything's been great."

Why is it always someone else, like the person next door, who gets to teach your kid to swim? Probably for the same reason that it's difficult to teach your spouse to drive. You're too close to the situation, and your anxiety or impatience impacts your desire to help them learn. But it doesn't have to be that way. Whether you are the parent, a neighbor, or a friend, you can be like the person who was your secret, most-loved adult when you were a kid.

How can you achieve the high status of becoming a child's favorite adult? How can you become like your favorite aunt or uncle—the ones you loved to visit because they were always so much fun and because you knew they weren't simply pretending to enjoy your company? Simple. Start by understanding that the rules of schmooze for adults also apply to kids. And that has to come from the parents first. You have to become the first line of defense. Laying down great self-esteem and moral goodness and, of course, schmoozing your kids with love, they will learn what you set down for them as their first role models.

So where do all your efforts start to go awry? I think I know. Did you ever see a movie called the "Groove Tube"? If not, rent it, because there's more fact than fiction here. One scene in the movie is a good tongue-in-cheek example of a major problem today. In the scene, a clown on a TV program has the kids send all the Moms and Dads out of the room. He then stops his high-pitched obnoxious voice, lights a cigarette, and tells the kids, "don't worry, no one is watching here either, so let's pick up where we left off last week." He then begins to read from *Lady Chatterley's Lover*, "his hand slowly roamed down the inside of her thigh."

While this is a big laugh part of the movie, now it's not so humorous, because that's what's going on in your living room today, even in the cartoons—and that's not funny. You have to harshly govern that would-be electric baby-sitter called television. But the solution to this is an easy one—all you have to do is turn it off. The hell with the V-chip, use the Off-chip. The only savior here is PBS and your own selected video tapes. Try as you might, you cannot, however, censor what they hear in school. When my daughter, Zsajsha, went to her first week of kindergarten, she came home and asked her mother, "Do you have to have sex before you get married?" This from a five-year-old who didn't have a clue of what sex was. Well, that's what you have to deal with.

SCHMOOZING FOR ALL AGES

When you schmooze a kid, you are also schmoozing the kid's parents. It's not that you set out specifically to do that, it just naturally happens. Every parent will see you as an extraordinary human being if you show interest in the family and really do enjoy their pride and joy. Let them know how good-looking and bright their kids are. Positive reinforcement pays off here, and you're not BSing them. You may just be talking about a future president. You see, I have no idea if my kids are good-looking. How could I? I love them too much to notice. But a good example of schmoozing parents by schmoozing kids is the dentist who sends a rattle (in the shape of a toothbrush with real bristles) to his client's newborns as a gift. He wins the parents' hearts and begins building a relationship with the child from day one. He or she has joined the family care team.

I have a special repertoire of jokes, riddles, and simple magic tricks and always keep at least one in my pocket, just for kids. I also make sure to stay in touch with the newest "rage," including new toys, cartoons, movies, and songs so I can talk "kid" with them. But schmoozing kids can be tricky, especially if their grandparents shower them with gifts and, as a result, they've come to expect them. It will take a little more thought to schmooze kids that you perceive are spoiled by material goods; the ones that greet you with their hands open instead of their arms. As a matter of fact, those "What didya bring me?" kind of kids may appreciate you more if you pay attention to them in a way that they may not be used to. Your time can be a gift; telling them a joke or a story can be a gift; or listening to them tell a joke (and laughing as if you've just heard it for the first time) can be a gift. Kids are smart. They know when they are being "bought off" and when they are being loved and acknowledged for who they are.

So, how do you schmooze a kid? The first thing you have to ask yourself is, "Do I like kids?" If you said no, then you might be just like "Eddie the Inch" (the nickname the neighborhood kids gave to the man who lived next door to me because he would never give them a fraction of an inch. Actually, what they called him was much worse, but let's stick with "Eddie the Inch"). Eddie was a sourpuss and hated the sight and sound of kids. He would yell at them and wouldn't let them cut across his yard or swim on "his" side of the lake. Although he was mean, we weren't, and so he was always invited to the neighborhood yard parties...if only he had wanted to join in the fun. If only he knew how much easier his life would have been if he had been willing to schmooze the neighborhood kids...

If you truly don't like kids, then ask yourself this next question, "Were you ever a kid?" If you answered no, then you've just learned why you probably have little or no affinity for them, since it's the kid in you that likes and can relate to the kid in them. If you want to be an all-around schmoozer, not just a specific-segment-of-the-population schmoozer, then you have to make a choice. Either stay as far away from those "little persons of tomorrow" as you can, or start schmoozing kids until you uncover that playful part of yourself that was somehow unfortunately squelched or forgotten. I encourage you to choose the latter—after all, who really wants be an "Eddie the Inch"? What's more, he died before his time.

I'm going to assume that you like kids and that your motives are pure. I'm going to assume that if you are a parent, you are already doing a lot of great things for your child or children. But, I am not going to assume that you are schmoozing them. Most parents either don't feel as though there's a need or don't think that they have the time. Neither could be further from the truth.

Schmoozing children is one step above raising them. It's respecting them. It's becoming a role model for them, so that they, in turn, will know how to schmooze the people in their lives (including you in your old age). Many children today say that they love their parents, but will they drive them to their Seniors' Club if it threatens to disrupt their busy lives? A true schmoozer will drive their parents and their parent's friends to the matinee and then take them all out to lunch when they are through. If you want to be more than just "tolerated" in your old age, teach your kids the value of schmoozing, and you'll not only have their love, but their friendship for life.

When I schmooze kids, I generally like to do it after they've done something nice, in order to reinforce their good behavior. If children are acknowledged for their good behavior, they are more likely to continue to behave positively, whether it is learning, helping with chores, or just being your pal. Realizing that whatever one does for thirty days tends to become a habit, my wife and I are using this awareness of habit-making to help my two daughters develop into responsible young women. Every morning, Zsajsha, who is now seven years old, makes her bed, puts the silverware from the dishwasher away, brushes her teeth, and puts her clothes in the hamper. For every day she finishes her chores, we put a star on her "chores" calendar.

At the end of each week, as a reward for completing her tasks, she gets to choose a gift that is in a "grab basket" of toys that my wife bought on sale (some are gift-wrapped and some are unwrapped). She knows that if she is irresponsible, the basket doesn't come out of the closet. And through this method of rewarding, Zsajsha has also learned the subtle lesson that the best gifts aren't always in the biggest boxes. A 98 cent toy, once a week, is a cheap price to pay for helping a child form good habits that could very well last a lifetime. Plus, it's fun on Saturday morning watching her choose from her toy basket. Zsajsha is now running that calendar for her two-year old sister, Z'dra.

Some wise man once said that all a man has to do for his children is love their mother. How could I not love my wife? She's so much better a person and a parent than I am, just by her nature. She humbles me. She spends her whole evening putting the two girls to bed, who she affectionately calls, "girlfriends." By reading to them, cuddling them, and making a big deal out of it when I come in to kiss them goodnight, she is dedicated to spending this part of her life in their youth. I often tell her, "wait, they'll blame you." She laughs and replies, "you're probably right, but they'll have the guilt that they deserve." Please forgive me for a time out here folks, but Annie, I dearly love you.

But our rewards aren't all materially based. With my children, I've rewarded them by spending extra time putting them to bed, or I've made up a new song with their names in it (and sometimes it even rhymes) or asked them if there was something they would like from me or would like me to do. Sometimes all they want is an extra long hug. When kids are given the freedom to choose the treat, they are "rewarding" themselves for their own behavior. This is actually a very subtle form of goal setting, and I've found that this "reward and recognition" attitude becomes internalized and continues throughout their lives as a form of self-acknowledgment. I would even go so far as to predict that the children who are schmoozed will be more likely to recognize and reward others for a job well done because they have a very clear sense of its value. Life must be more than learning the three R's. It also must include the Three R's of Schmoozing: Recognition, Reward, and Rejoicing.

I would also add another "R" word to this list, and that word is "ritual." Ritual is a great way to connect with kids, to show them you care, and to demonstrate there is a level of consistency that they can trust. Every night, when I put Zsajsha to bed, we have a ritual where we give each other a "hugglebuggle," which simply means that we hug, rub noses together, give each other a high five, a low five, and a kiss. When I travel, in order to stay connected with her, we continue our bedtime ritual, but over the phone. She cradles the phone and gives it a hug, she rubs her nose on it, then she gives the ear piece a high five, the mouthpiece a low five, and finally blows a kiss into the phone. When I'm halfway across the globe and just waking up, I put her to sleep with our ritual, and when she is waking up and I am off to bed, she uses our ritual to send me off to sleep. As she grows up, our rituals no doubt will change, but the importance of creating and sustaining them will remain.

I choose to raise my kids in this way to be the best of the end of my DNA, simply to break the chain of abuse that I received from my parents as a child. My parents used a "pitta" (a Russian word that means punishment) to keep us in line. A pitta was a belt that had been cut into small strips and attached to a piece of wood—in essence, a homemade cat-o-nine tails. Unfortunately, this tradition was passed down through generation after generation, and they actually thought this was right. I swore to myself that I would not carry on that tradition with my children, no matter how bad their behavior was. One thing our children will be able to say is that "my parents never laid a glove on us."

If you're a single parent, never, let me say that again, never let your new spouse do the disciplining, and absolutely no physical discipline. I talk from experience here. To a kid, this is the biggest betrayal they will ever experience. They will never forget. Bite the bullet. Tell your new partner that you'll handle the discipline. It will make it easier for the child to accept the new partner, and easier on the partner if the child is not resentful. Hey, if you listen to the news, most of the time when a child is beaten to death, it's by a stepparent or a boyfriend or girlfriend. In the animal kingdom, when lions, gorillas, or elephants take over a pride—and this is a fact—their first job is to kill off the DNA of the fallen pride leader. You can work with your new partner on behavior, but let the new partner be the good cop.

Extra Effort and Sky Lab

When my oldest, Todd, was seven, Sky Lab was continually in the news because its orbit was disintegrating and the scientists were predicting that it was going to crash into the Earth. For three weeks, Todd and I collected all the data from the newspaper for a scrapbook, or anything else we could hear on TV about Sky Lab's inevitable breakup. The night before it was to plummet to Earth, the newspaper showed a picture of the route it was going to take. Luckily, it landed in the Atlantic Ocean, but only after it had cut its path across our state. I knew that after all this excitement, a climactic ending was called for, so I went to Nick Herrol's junkyard and found an old pump with pipes, knobs, a pulley, and a large wheel attached.

Todd had invited his friend John Pesicek to sleep over on the night that Sky Lab was going to crash to Earth. At midnight, I took this huge pump, raised it over my head, and threw it into the lawn. I gathered several tubes that glow when you shake and break them and dropped them, along with lit cigarettes, into the pipes so the metal glowed and smoked. Then I went back into the house, jumped on the floor, ran down the stairs, and yelled, "What was that?" When the boys woke up, I told them that I had heard a big crash and asked them if they thought it might be a part of Sky Lab. I had three flashlights ready, and together we went outside to investigate. I kept shining my light anywhere but on the pump so that they would be the ones to discover the "crash site."

When they finally discovered this heap of glowing and smoking metal, they were awestruck. I walked over to it and pretended it was too hot to touch and then said, "Well, we have two choices—we can call the police and they'll take it, or we can run a board through the wheel and carry it to the garage so we can take it apart tomorrow." They opted to carry it to the garage, and I'm sure they didn't sleep much that evening. The next day, I photographed the event as they were taking apart the piece of junk lying on the morning newspaper headlines "Skylab Crashes."

Three years later, when we were looking at the photos, Todd asked, "Did Sky Lab really fall into our backyard?" At that point, I had to level with him. Todd couldn't believe that I would put forth so much effort just to make the Sky Lab event memorable for him. I know he secretly enjoyed it, and I'm sure he'll tell his kids stories about the evening that the Sky Lab fell—and he'll have the photos to prove it.

Maybe some of you are saying to yourself, "I would never go through that much trouble just to make an impression on a child." My response to that comment is...if you don't go through the trouble for your kids early on, you'll probably have to go through trouble with your kids later. The problem now is that you view the extra effort as going through "trouble." The busier you keep your kids, and the more involved you keep them in things like music, arts, athletics, jobs, and volunteering, the less time they will have to get involved with dirtballs. The advantage is that all of the above come with values, and when they reach their teens, no dirtball will be able to compete with that and lead them astray. For example, not only do I not think it's trouble to take my daughter to a movie, but I don't just drop her off at the theater, I let her bring a friend, and I go to see the movie with them. The movie becomes an outing, and at the end of the day, because the experience is shared together, there's no need to ask, "So honey, what fun thing did you do today?" This willingness to put your kids first creates "low-maintenance" kids in the long run. For as long as you can, enjoy their childhood *with* them, because sooner than you think, they're not going to want you to come along anymore.

Schmoozing the Neighborhood Kids

There is much truth to the saying that it takes a great village (or neighborhood) to raise great kids. The Kid Schmooze is important, especially if they are neighborhood kids, because they will be living near you for a long time, or what will seem like a long time if you don't get to know them. That's why I pay close attention to all the kids that are within my sphere of influence and make them a special part of my life—I want to build a strong neighborhood, not strong neighbor "hoods." For example, in my garage, I have life-size cutout pictures of former Milwaukee Brewers Robin Yount and Paul Molitor. The captions on them read, "Can you measure up?" Every year at Christmas, I have the neighborhood kids stand next to the cutout, I take a picture, and on the picture, I write their name, the date, and how much they've grown. Years down the line, this will serve as a nice piece of history for them.

Whenever I did concrete work in my yard, I invited the neighborhood kids over to put their hand prints into the concrete, since I know what a strong lure wet concrete is for most kids. I'd rather invite playful behavior and be *delighted* than be on the receiving end of a prank and become *incited*. I also get groups of kids to play Pictionary, Dictionary, or Kid's Trivia and have campfires and sing-alongs for the same reason. As a volunteer fireman, I know that kids are fascinated and naturally drawn to fire, so I would rather fulfill their desire to play with fire in a structured and supervised way than have to deal with a four-alarm fire because some kid was curious but irresponsible with matches.

One of my favorite ways to interact with the neighborhood kids was to ring a bell I had hung outside. This was my "trick or treat" bell. When the bell rang, the kids would come running into my yard to see if I was going to deliver a "trick" or a "treat." Of course, I always picked tricks that were fair. One of my tricks on a hot day was to ring the bell and then duck out of sight. When they got to my porch, they sometimes discovered water balloons, and other times, a water pail and squirt guns. After they grabbed their weapons, I appeared as the amazing "Unwettable Man," complete with terry cloth towel cape, mask, and squirting "machine gun" (only because the odds were stacked in their favor), and we had a wonderful squirt gun fight.

There were hot days in the summer that I would declare National Popsicle or Ice Cold Watermelon Day, and I'd hand everyone a cool treat. In October, I would have a contest for the best Halloween costume, and everyone would receive a small prize—I never got tricks because our house was a treat. Occasionally, I'd take out my Polaroid camera and have "The Best Funny Face Contest" (Stevie Vento always won), with each child receiving the silly photograph. Another variation on this theme was to visit the kindergartens and help the teacher put clown make-up on the kids. We photographed each of them and put the photos in an album. To this day, many of the students will come back to visit the school just to see their picture and reminisce, and I still put on the make-up to this day.

One Christmas, with the help of the neighborhood parents, I bought presents and set up a scavenger hunt. All the kids went door to door looking for clues. They sang carols to get the clues and finally arrived at my house only to discover that their parents were there too. We gave them the gifts and had a wonderful indoor winter block party. Our neighborhood has also created a tradition of playing a game called "Christmas Greed" during the Christmas holidays. Each person gift wraps and brings a special item that they no longer want to the party, except for the host who "salts the pot" by buying and wrapping several nice items that will make the game more interesting. Everyone shakes a pair of dice, and if they get a three or a nine, they get to choose a present from the pile that is in the middle of the floor. Everyone continues to shake until all the presents are distributed. Then, the gifts are opened, and you see who has had the luck to get the "hot" presents. A timer is then set for five minutes, and everyone gets a chance to roll the dice again. This time, if you roll a three or a nine, you get to *take* a present from anyone you want. You can keep rolling and taking gifts if you keep getting threes or nines, but if you roll other than those two numbers, you have to pass the dice to the next person. After five minutes, when the timer goes off, whatever gifts you end up with are yours to keep. There is so much laughter generated that everyone wins, no matter who ends up with the tangible presents. On Christmas Day, our kids must pick out three presents they are willing to give up, and then we drive to the food kitchen in the city, where the entire family dons aprons to serve turkey and mashed potatoes in the food line. And we do it on non-holidays as well. It ain't much, but I believe my babies are better for it.

Most of the neighborhood kids are grown now, and I don't ring the "trick or treat" bell very often anymore. But I'm hoping that a whole new gang of little kids moves into my neighborhood so I can start all over again, as now I have two young ones of my own.

TIPS, TRICKS, AND RESOURCES

This section is for your practical side. This is the side that needs some quick tips for creative schmooze ideas, inexpensive crafts and gifts, or just needs to know what to pick out on your next trip to the bookstore. So here goes...

All my children have had and will continue to have access to music videos–and I'm not referring to the rock videos of MTV. Zsajsha has a video collection of over fifty musicals, and every Saturday morning, she chooses which video she wants to see, and we watch it together. Even though many of the musicals are dated, they still contain valuable lessons about honesty, kindness, and love. I would rather they see visions of virtue and loveliness than visions of violence and lovelessness, no matter how "dated" the material may seem to the modern eye.

This is also true of the books we read together. Every child deserves a bookshelf of their very own, filled with books that help them discover who they are and who they are capable of becoming. One of my favorite examples of this type of book is *Positively Mother Goose*, published by H.J. Kramer. The old rhymes are printed on the front and back covers and the "reframed rhymes," which just means they aren't distorted or bizarre, are beautifully illustrated. I am always on the lookout for uplifting and positive books, from the classics like *My Secret Garden*, *The Little Princess*, and *The Princess Bride*, to recently published books such as *Old Turtle*, or the one I'm writing as we speak, *Three Rocks High*. One of my favorite gifts to give to a child is a book. But an even greater gift is the time one spends reading it with them.

There are also many great resource books that give valuable ideas for activities that parents can do together with their children. *Kid's Random Acts of Kindness I & II* are two such wonderful books. *Full Esteem Ahead*, written by Diane Loomans and her daughter, Julia, is a great book for those of you who want to become the dream parent that perhaps you never had, and my favorite book is *You're a Good Dog Carl*. You do not have to raise your children the way you were raised, unless you had a wonderful family life. Because my upbringing was less than ideal, I do everything I can for and with my children, hoping to break the cycle of poor parenting. There's always room for improvement—even in the raising of children.

One of the critical rules of schmoozing children is to understand and honor your place and your relationship with them and their parents. Some of these ideas are for parents only. Others are for relatives and blood relations, and others for close friends. Please be sensitive and do not overstep your boundaries since you can do more damage to the relationship than good. As you go through this list, find one thing that really seems like a great idea, and try it. You'll be surprised that there is always more to learn and more ways to love than you might have considered. For more ideas beyond this list, get the book called *365 Afterschool Activities: TV Free Fun for Kids Age 7–12* by Sheila Ellison and Judith Gray. Here are some ideas to get you started, you may find one you'll like:

- When visiting the parents of a child, take out a small item you have purchased especially for them, but begin playing with it as if it's yours. Then let them play with it while you visit. Before you leave…give it to the child for being a cool new friend while you were visiting.

- Never bring a gift (for the kids) that will be so messy that the parents will wish you hadn't come to visit.

- Learn a craft such as origami either with the child or to teach to them later.

- Get a "Cat in the Cradle" book and some yarn. If you teach this game to someone you visit, you'll always have that in common with them. And yes, boys like it too.

- Plan a picnic with an alternative rain site, such as a roller rink or a movie theater.

- Teach them to catch and release fireflies or any other creatures and critters. At bird feed stores, they have wonderful cages made of screen with a magnifying glass for a door. Buy a hummingbird feeder or regular bird feeder. Give animals a personality and make sure that the child understands that the animal, reptile, or insect has a mother and father too and wants to go home to their family.

- Give a less fortunate kid in the neighborhood a job in your yard as an excuse to finance them for their needs and lead as an example and a role model. You will receive unsuspected rewards in the future.

- If you can afford to, rent or buy a battery-run VCR/TV with tapes for all those road trips. The best of all worlds is one with earphones so you can pay attention to the road, or if one of the kids wants to sleep.

- Make up a bedtime story, or read one to your child, and then use your child's name in place of the major character in the story. Make up a pleasant story, and use it as an alternate dream for your child. Then if your child has a nightmare, you can use the "good" dream as a substitution for the bad one. Works every time.

- Teach your kid to be the champion of the underdog kids in the neighborhood.

- Get on the mailing list of your local zoo and museums, and call your state's travel and tourism office to request their Calendar of Events. Allow your child to choose one event a week or month that they want to do. Let them help you plan the outing.

- Let your child stay up late one night and spend the time counting the stars or looking at the moon. Or, wake them up if you get home late just to count the stars. They will think getting up, if only briefly, at this forbidden hour is very special.

- Take your kid to one of those guaranteed catch-a-fish places; not only will you create a healthy pastime, but you will hook him or her into eating fish—the best source on earth for niacin.

- If you don't have kids, sign up to be a Big Brother or Big Sister. Find organizations that need adult sponsors or chaperones for kids, and volunteer your time.

- Talk with your child's teacher and pre-arrange to have pizzas sent to your child's class for their birthday, special occasion, no occasion, or if your child is entering a new school. Ask the teacher what the school's policy is for visiting, and then occasionally stop in to visit your child's school and class.

- Use any holiday as an excuse to set up a treasure hunt. Have a few kids help you create the clues. Challenge them to write the clues in rhyming verse.

- If you have a tree in your yard, put up a tire swing or a tree house, but make it low to the ground so no one gets hurt.

- Send your kids to acting, karate, or computer camp, or any camp that supports their interests. For fun, check out Circus Smirkus from your travel agent, a summer camp that teaches circus skills for a month then goes out and performs them in the big top.

- Every year, whether in the city or country, plant some kind of edible vegetable or fruit so the child can watch it grow and then enjoy eating what it produces, even if you have to grow them in a five-gallon bucket on your windowsill.

- If you travel, try to find your child a pen pal from a foreign country your child is interested in.

- If you have a home video camera, make a video where your child is the star. For example, one of my daughter's favorite videos is an adventure that included her two cousins in the story. Zsajsha buries a treasure chest in the garden, and her cousins find it, only to discover there's nothing in it. Meanwhile, she buries the "real" treasure in another spot. Be willing to play cameraman for a day, and let them write and direct their own home movie.

- When vacationing, buy everyone a disposable camera. Later, hold a photo contest where everyone judges the best photo from the trip. Also, try this one: write your names on the top of disposable cameras, and exchange them with partners. Then take candid shots of each other. When these shots are developed, it's a scream to see what the kids were up to.

- Show your child how to use a tape recorder, and let them experiment with it.

- Stop at rummage sales and buy all the junk jewelry you can. Then wash it off with alcohol, put it in a box that looks like a treasure chest, and let them play with it.

- Buy a bucket of water-soluble paint or chalk. Draw a giant map of the United States or the world on your driveway and create a game with them to help them learn about the states and their capitals.

- Go to rummage sales or resale shops just to look for toys or fun things for kids. Sometimes you can find treasures from parents whose kids are grown, like a rock polishing kit, flower press, or ant farm.

- Buy the crystal growing kit at a store that sells nature items. It's a great way to have fun and learn in the process!

- Warn them ahead of time what it is going to be like to be a teen. As a teenager, they may think that their parents are stupid and embarrassing, but it's just their hormones causing them to act this way. Now that they know, ask them to take it easy on you.

- After you take a vacation, make a family scrapbook or photo-story of the trip. Make it funny by having the kids write in the captions.

- When they are young, play night vision games where they close their eyes for thirty seconds and then try to spot things in the dark. Also try playing nighttime hide-and-go-seek. It may help them to be unafraid of the dark.

- For safety, teach them, and actually practice with them, an alternate escape route from the house or apartment in case there's a fire.

- When you are out of town, always send your kids postcards. And if you don't have kids, get the address of nieces, nephews, or your favorite friend's kids, and send them a postcard. Kids love to get their own mail.

- Don't ever buy a "pet" for a child, whether a turtle, rabbit, ferret, or an iguana, without asking the parent's permission first. (And if it's for your kid, don't forget to check with your spouse first.)

- If you have a pet (such as a hamster or goldfish) that dies and the child is too little to understand death, go to the store and replace it. For the very young, you don't need to introduce a trauma they won't understand no matter how much you explain it. Tell them it was just sleeping. Once they are old enough and can deal with the death of a pet, make sure to give the pet a proper burial (toilet not optional).

- Teach kids games, songs, or how to whistle.

- Spend quiet time alone with them, specifically to talk with your Creator and give thanks for all the good stuff you have.

- If you find a reasonably priced microscope or telescope, buy it. Kids love 'em.

- Have a game drawer filled with card games and board games that they have access to when they are bored.

- Try not to use the television as an electronic baby-sitter.

- Have a signal, such as a whistle, to help keep track of your child when in a crowd. When your child hears the whistle, he or she has to come back to you and say "I'm here."

- Buy a small whistle for your kids to wear around their neck, and teach them to respond to your whistle with their own.

- Teach your child how and when to dial 911. Then explain that only a very small child would ever dial that number without reason. Because the child will want to be considered "older," they will use 911 only when needed.

- Get a reasonable set of walkie-talkies for outings (or just for fun) or give one to the kid next door, it will keep them off the phone.

- Start a kazoo Christmas caroling band. That way you don't have to know the words.

- Take a swimming course with your kids, even when they are babies.

- Call their names for no reason. When they answer, say "I love you."

- Teach them how to say "I love you" using American Sign Language. It's thumb out, little finger and pointing finger pointing up and two middle fingers down. When you wiggle your pointing finger up and down it means "very much." Use that signal with them whenever you want to express your love to them, especially from a distance or in a crowd.

- Try this poem with the little ones: "Do you love me or do you not? You told me once but I forgot." They will invariably respond with, "Yes, I love you."

- Never go into any large crowds without giving your child an ID bracelet or at least your phone number written inside of his or her shoe.

• Play simple games of blackjack with them with all cards face-up, and use chips. Your kids will be exceptional in math if they have to do the addition for both of you to see who won each hand and be the bank with the chips.

• Make a "correct answer" penny bank with two bowls of pennies and then use flash cards or smart cards before bed. When they get a question right, they get a penny. When they get one wrong, you take a penny back. Then ask the question again three cards later as a review, and if they get it right, give the penny back again plus another.

• With very little kids, squat or physically move so you can actually make eye contact with them. With very shy kids, don't move too fast and don't make direct eye contact right away. Give them time to accept you.

• Before your family's inevitable trip to Washington DC, write your Congressperson at least one month beforehand to let him or her know when you will be there. You will be amazed at the packet of perks you will receive for his constituent.

• Never force a child to hug or kiss someone they don't want to. Instead whisper to them, "If you want to give Uncle Tommy a hug, you can," and then let them make the choice. More often than not, they will choose to give that special person a hug.

• Ask parents prior to giving their child candy or treats.

• Make a face mask of your own face with Vaseline and plaster bandages (the instructions for this technique can be found in most art stores). Once you have a mold, pour concrete in the masks and make a face that can then be put into the flower garden. Make a concrete face for each member of the family.

• Let your oldest child know that his or her job is to teach the younger sibling. Reward them when you see them doing their job well.

• Keep your eyes open for outings or events that are designed for families.

• If you don't have kids, volunteer to baby-sit for your friends for an evening. They'll get a break from their routine, and you'll have a treat being with their children.

• When eating out at a restaurant, bring a small bag of crayons and some blank scrap paper (in case the dining establishment doesn't have paper place mats). Draw on the paper, beginning with an oval shape, and pass the paper or place mat back and forth with the goal of drawing a face. Continue to add elements until the face is ridiculous or until dinner is served.

• Buy a book with guessing games, and keep it with you for those times when you are traveling or dining out.

• Take the official tour of any cities that you visit together. It's an interesting way to learn about the geography of that city, relax a little, and keep everyone interested. When it comes up in school, they will know about it firsthand.

• Encourage your child to have a pen pal with any kid they befriend when they are at camp or on vacation.

• For the little ones just learning to read, label everything in their room (chair, table, bed, etc....) with large, colorful printed cards. They will learn to read more quickly.

• Use the footprint or handprint kit to make a special clay memento of their first few days. On the back, write their name, the date, a special message to them such as, "I've talked to the Governor, and you'll grow," and then sign it and bake it.

- Go to a trophy store and get a "best sister" or "best brother" trophy. Do this especially for the older sibling, and make a big deal of it so they have a sense of pride about their role in the family.

- Think of someone in your life that was the kindest to you or taught you the most. If they are deceased, close your eyes and say "thank-you." If they are still alive, give them a call and let them know how important they are to you. Do it now.

- And the most important of all, create and demand family unity.

- Finally, here's a secret writing code that you can share with your favorite young person. This is a very special way to leave notes for one another. Let's say you were going to spell "Dorothy." Use parts from the graph to identify each letter. Note that some parts of the graph have dots in them, some don't. Each letter can be identified by the lines immediately framing it, and whether it has a dot in it or not. If you feel someone has figured out your code, you can move your alphabet around within the graph anytime you'd like. If you look at it, its pretty easy to figure it out. If you're having a hard time, get a kid to show you how to do it.

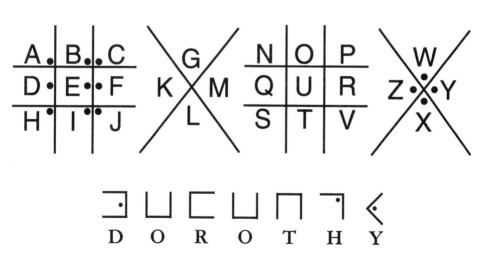

CHAPTER SIXTEEN

TEEN SCHMOOZING

Saving the Rebels without a Clue

Here's the good news—the kid that gives you the most gray hairs will be the one that will come back to take care of you in your old age. The bad news is that you can only hope the kid isn't creating his own "Home Shopping Network" in stranger's homes.

Where was I when I needed me as a teenager? Luckily for my mother, when I hit my teens, I left home and went to live with relatives on the carnival circuit. But I know I gave her my share of gray hairs before I left. When she told me that only the good die young, it just encouraged me. I was the biggest possible jerk I could be. But there are a few things that might at least let me off the hook a little for my behavior.

First, my father died when I was eleven. Before he died, he really didn't have a lot of time to teach me any of the social graces that I dearly needed. I can't blame him. And the four years prior to his death, my parents were very involved with my sister who was dying of cancer of the mouth. It was a no-win battle that turned two people who never drank into alcoholics.

I can't help thinking to myself that perhaps some of you who are reading this might be thinking, yeah, when I was a teenager, I was a jerk too.

Well, aren't we all at some time? Oh, and by the way, if you're about my age and your bike was stolen when you were young, I'm sorry.

THE MINISTRY

I'm not very religious, although I talk to God daily. I do have a ministry, however—I teach kids magic and comedy. I generally take kids that remind me of myself in my youth. When I was young, I liked kids that had wonderful homes and great parents, and I envied them too. Today, I'm great to everybody's Mom and Dad, and moms and dads pick up on that. They can tell that I have a special like for them simply because they're good parents. Unfortunately, I had to learn social skills and the rules of schmoozing on my own, and I often stumbled along the way. If I can avoid that for anybody else, I'll give it a wholehearted try.

There are at least a dozen young people who are now in their thirties who I brought up in the ministry of what I know—show business. As a matter of fact, for a recent reward, one of the Will Rogers of our time, comic Will Durst (you may have seen him on TV during presidential elections or heard him on National Public Radio), stated in a book that he owed his career to me. I was duly flattered, especially since I know he will be an even bigger star in the future. Thanks Will.

So before I start telling you how to schmooze teens, let me say this. If you felt you didn't catch a break as a teen, and now you're an adult who is able to give one, please do so. Make it your ministry. It can be in anything that you're good at that will catch their interest, take them off the streets, and head them in the right direction. Saving a human being is one of the most blessed things you can do in a lifetime. In the words of King Arthur, "by serving one another, we are free."

I have put my money where my mouth is. Instead of the more faceless giving of money to charity, I have purchased clothing for kids I knew, or braces for their teeth. I've given them magic props and connected them with their first job. I've also summoned friends of mine who could render their services to help the kids out (thanks Vic Thomas and David Seebach). I've also approached groups like the Lions or Lionesses, Optimists, Eagles, or the Rotarians to have them focus on somebody in their own backyards who needed some extra love and attention. I also find that retired teachers are often willing to tutor a kid who is behind in school.

No, I'm not Ghandi—I'm more guilty. In my youth, I lead a total survival lifestyle, because I was illiterate and in trouble with the law. So today, if I can catch a kid a break, I'm more than glad to do it. I've paid for workshops and talked kids' ways into schools, colleges, and even summer jobs. But it isn't 100 percent science.

There will be kids that you won't be able to pull out of the fire with a pair of tongs. They just refuse to get it. If it were raining soup, they'd be standing outside with a fork! But I'm proud to reveal that those are the minority. And here's the reward. Here's how you and the seemingly minor amount of assistance you give to just a few kids can improve the world. The only demands made on the kids I worked with was that one day they had to teach ten more. Today, those kids are now adults and close, beloved friends of mine, and they are each spreading a ministry of their own. So far, the winner is a very successful and probably one of the best voice-over guys in the U.S., named C.W. Wolfe. He's paid back the ten he owes me, and he's added one hundred on top of that number.

SCHMOOZING OTHERS' TEENS
You can see talent in teens. All things being equal when you're a teen, the thing that you most think about being is actually what you would most like to be. Start there—ask them that question. And even if it's preposterous, let them go for it. It's the only way they'll find out, and wouldn't *you* be surprised if they pull it off? For example, one summer I had an intern working with me at Milwaukee Summerfest, named Amy

Pietz. At the time, she was about sixteen years old. I asked her, "Where are you in five years?" In less than a heartbeat, she answered, "On TV." Well, she wasn't talking just to hear herself, as she recently won an award for her role on *Caroline in the City*. She had it all—she was bright and polite, but more than that, she was focused and knew where she was going and what she wanted. I had little to do with her career. It was only about two weeks, but I am looking at a log entry of mine from that time that reads, "Amy Pietz will happen." Five out of the eight times I have written that down in my log, it has happened. I am waiting for Chris Barnes, Lukeski, Darrell Hammond, Eric O'Shea, Scott Henry, and Monica Carter. If there's anything to them, it will show up in their eyes. All you need to do is ask, "how can I help?" I have worked with skinheads, dopers, thieves, and underachievers. Only a few have fallen by the wayside. All the rest are working somewhere in the entertainment industry.

Let's start with schmoozing a teen that is not your teen. This is just a kid in your neighborhood who's giving you a lot of gas, or God forbid, a gang situation. I don't really know anybody who wants to be in that gang situation, but if you're on the receiving end of a harassment problem, you had better deal with it quickly or move. Those are your only two options. With moving being so expensive, I suggest you try talking to the kid, and the best place to do this is in front of one of his parents. You'll be surprised sometimes at the turnaround of the result. Be understanding and diplomatic in talking about the situation. Make him or her know that it is truly a misunderstanding, which should defuse any problem you may have in the future with this kid.

Next, if you want to be a nice guy and a big brother who puts this kid under your wing, offer him some work. There may be something you have to do around the house, such as painting, cleaning up, or maybe yard work. This will give the kid an opportunity to get to know you and find some kind of bond. Generally, a good hook is to offer him a couple bucks over minimum wage. All of a sudden, you have a relationship.

You become an advisor. You may end up with a very old friend years down the road.

Or you can try using a little psychology. In my hometown, every night a group of kids would gather on the stoop of a local business. They were breaking windows, writing graffiti, and leaving it a mess. Pat, the guy who owned the business, kept confronting the kids, but that would only encourage them to mess with him. One night, I suggested to him that he take a case of soft drinks over, tell them that whoever cleaned up the mess the night before had done a nice job, that he really appreciated it, and that he didn't mind them sitting there anymore. Also, he said that he was wrong about them in the first place and asked them to please accept his apology.

Two things happened: First, they bought it, and he never had a problem with them again. Second, they left his stoop and went someplace else. I don't think they could live up to being good guys. Seems like an extortion racket for soda water? Maybe, but it worked. And if you figure that all it cost was a case of soda, that's great, because the alternative could have been a lot more damage. You've got to remember that *no one* wants kids around when they're teens. Industry doesn't want them. Insurance doesn't want them. Their schools barely want them. The only people that should want them are their loving parents, which a lot of time they don't have. That's where you may come in handy.

Schmoozing Your Own

First, if you're a parent, I don't care if you're a single parent, it is important that you start Teen Schmoozing between the ages of six and ten (if you don't, you're already heading for trouble). Let them know that when they hit puberty, their hormones are going to be slam dancing with their brains. My belief is that taking away stigmas from "big deal" things like drinking and smoking at those ages will defuse their interest when they get offered those dummy pleasures in an alley or behind the garage.

For my son Todd's fifth birthday, I gave him a six-pack of Billy Carter beer, a pouch of Red Man chewing tobacco, a pack of unfiltered Pall Malls, and a tin of Copenhagen snuff. His friends were amazed when they came over. They would say, "don't you have to hide that stuff?" His answer, of course, was, "No, my dad *gave* me that." Over the years, he eventually tried all of it except the Red Man chewing tobacco (he had had enough with the Copenhagen snuff). By the time he tried one of the unfiltered Pall Malls, they were so dried out that it was a truly awful experience. As he grew into his teen years, the youthful fascination with tobacco, alcohol, and drugs was gone. Been there, done that. I still don't know if it was the fact that he was able to unsuccessfully, even sickeningly, try those things, or the fact that there was nobody saying, "Hey you can't have that—and don't you ever let me catch you with it."

I remember being a hungry child. We had no food around the house. A friend of mine, Doug, came over one day and said, "hey, I've got a quart of beer." I replied, "my refrigerator is full of beer. Do you have any food?" Doug had those parents that said "don't you ever, ever touch a drop of alcohol," and that's the behavior it bred. If you think about it, parents who were really uptight about their kids drinking were the parents doing all the drinking. And in most of those cases, the parents were preaching from a hypocritical pulpit—they drank and smoked as well. Think about it. Perhaps you can spring the luring trap of tobacco and alcohol by taking away the bait of stigma. Fact: according to experts, if parents smoke, their kids are more likely to smoke—they're following their role models.

Now, if your own kids are heading for trouble and you haven't done the proper turnarounds and warnings before they get there, and he or she doesn't look like the kid on the porch in *Deliverance*, there are still some ways you can save them. First, hit them where they're very vulnerable— where their interests are. If they have a negative interest, try to compare it to a good interest. For example, if they're getting into a lot of fights, and I know you'll think this is crazy, but believe me it works, enroll them in karate. I send my kids to Roufus Karate, not because Pat Roufus' kid is the heavyweight champion, but because they teach self-esteem as well as self-defense.

The better karate schools are made up of half martial arts and half self-esteem. Students are told from the start that their skills are never to be used against brothers, sisters, family members, or anybody just to show off their strength. It is only used for self-defense. One family I know had a young teen who was a low achiever in school and was heavily picked on by other kids. Soon after being enrolled in karate, his grades rose to where they were supposed to be, his popularity picked up, and he was no longer picked on. Within two years, he received his black belt and was offered a job as instructor at the same karate school he went to.

Talking to another parent, I learned how a girl in her early teens was suffering from bulimia and anorexia. She was also enrolled in karate. She soon learned to use food as energy for karate competition. One caveat here, though: if you try this route, you have to check to make sure the school you're enrolling your child in has a great self-esteem package accompanying it.

Another idea for a constructive activity you can get your kids into is summer camps where they get a chance to work helping handicapped kids. If you can't afford it, start calling these camps about volunteer opportunities, and don't wait until the eleventh hour. Start in January or February so your kids can get in. Being around good role models like the instructors at these camps can be wonderful for them. Also, McDonald's is one of the best jobs a kid can have. Today, operations like those and the U.S. Army are about the only ones teaching regimentation, courtesy, and good work ethics.

If you are fortunate enough to have a kid who's interested in the arts, encourage him and give him lessons, whether it be music, dance, or acting. For example, if you find your child is into graffiti, they may have a great art hand. Whether it be in writing, painting, or drawing, encourage it, and again, put your money where your mouth is. Put an art workshop into his life. When he has a choice of hanging out with the dirtballs or following his art, trust me, the dirtballs will fall short. He would rather be painting signs, detailing cars, or perhaps becoming the next Rembrandt. And if you think you can't afford it, turn to a Dutch Uncle to help you, and see if there are any grants or special programs around to make it possible. Also, remember that kids who are kept really busy in gymnastics, swimming, or sports of any kind seem to have a greater knack for staying out of trouble.

I also recommend a fantastic book on the subject that dedicates itself to ideas for how to keep your kids off drugs and what to do if they're already into them. It's called *When Saying No Isn't Enough*, by Ken Barun and Philip Base (published by Signet).

CHAPTER SEVENTEEN

SCHMOOZE YOURSELF
TO GOOD HEALTH

If You Think "Hygiene" Is a Greeting, You Need This Chapter

W hatever your beliefs are about creation—whether a supreme being casted a man, a woman, and a snake; we climbed out of the slime and muck; or we are some extraterrestrial's D-student kid's science project—we tend to forget our ancestry in that equation. In either your prayers or meditation, you have use of your 411 DNA directory. I think that DNA should stand for Deploying Networking Ancestry. For me, my mom was my hero, mentor, and champion. She was a four-letter word slinging, savvy carnie promoter, suckle a child on one breast and kill a man with her free hand type of woman. Short of the four-letter words, I married one just like her.

So when I get in a tough spot, I call on my mother and ask what she would do in the same spot. When the answer comes, just like in life, she's always right. I'm sure that you've done this with some past relative in your life. Who hasn't? The thought has led me to carry it even further. Think about it—your thousandth great grandmother and grandfather (the ones who lived in a cave) have DNA living in you today. They're alive and well in your unconscious. They're on the inside, and the inside only. And here we stand at the end of that DNA strand.

All you have to do to draw from that great pool of knowledge is to seclude yourself, meditate, and call upon your DNA index. Personally, I think it's bigger, better, and more powerful than the Internet. I do it all the time. Hell, someone in my ancestry is helping me tell you about them right now (I could never come up with this kind of stuff alone). The trick is that you have to ask for their advice to get it. Here's my key phrase when I'm asking: Hey Grand-Prophets (they're flattered by this), which one of you can help me out today with a problem I'm having with one of your grandkids? A present I want to get for your great-daughter-in-law? A horse trade I'm doing? A fear I'm dealing with? Something that's puzzling me?

They're in your head, your brain, your blood. They are there waiting for you to draw from them, and they're glad to do it because they love you and want to help, just like you would like to guide your offspring when you're gone. If you can't get a picture of this scenario in your mind, go pick up *Carousel* on video. It's corny, but you'll get the picture. Hey, I know it sounds like I'm over the top on this one, and I've tried to rationalize that it's just me, but I'm just not that smart. Sometimes I get answers that are not in my vocabulary, unless some offspring of Bill Maher and Dennis Miller are sneaking in.

When I get answers that surprise even myself, it's a prize every time, and when the right answer pops into my mind, I can somehow feel them smiling at me. I can feel the courageousness in each and every one of them. And I also get the feeling they are blocking a few of the dark-side relatives from influencing me. I'm sure we've all had a few Attila the Dumbs in our ancestry.

I draw my health, energy, and immunities from those in my ancestral chain. After all, they have had all these experiences before me. And for the record, I do not believe in channeling, especially if someone charges you for it (sorry, Ms. MacLaine). But when you think of the vested interest your DNA has in you, you cannot negate the endless possibilities of cures, preventions, and remedies they have collected over the centuries.

You are their living kid, the end of their strand to date, hoping you will be the best of all of them in deed and health. So give 'em a ring. What could it hurt?

MY MIXER ELIXIR

Schmoozing yourself to good health starts with a simple rule of life from Dr. Steven Covey, the author of *The Seven Habits of Highly Effective People*. My favorite quote from this book is, "Think of how you would like to be remembered at your funeral and use it as a basis for your everyday behavior." Let that sentence aid you as it aided me. It caused a very awakening within myself. To live better, I had to be better. It made me a better role model to my friends, my family, and my work mates. I've come a long way, baby.

I know a little bit about this material, because I'm a cancer survivor. Fourteen years ago, I was diagnosed with malignant rectal cancer. I like being popular, and it was nice to know that it was the most popular cancer in men in my age group (twenty-five to forty-five). At that time, my eating habits were atrocious. I was eating four or five porterhouse steaks a week, and I understand that undigested steak can remain in your intestines for as long as four or five months, especially if it's unground. (Sincerely, do you think I should be a dinner speaker so far?) And you wonder why your doctor wants you on a high fiber diet.

Allow me to be profound when I say that we take our health, our life, and our senses for granted every minute of every day. You don't really think about it until something shocking happens. My moment was when I found out I had malignant cancer. Let's go back to my moment of reckoning fourteen years ago. I was ignoring all the signs that told me something was wrong with me. I was about to go on a two-week vacation to the Caribbean, but the discomfort and pain forced me to see the doctor before I left. Had I left on that vacation, you wouldn't be reading this book right now.

The moment I knew I had cancer was not after I waited the long hours for the phone to ring with the biopsy results. It was when I was at my doctor's office, and he had me in that ungraceful position on a proctor table. Having completed his examination, my doctor brought in another doctor in the hospital for his opinion. Straight ahead of me in the examining office was a glass case with instruments in it. I could see both of their reflections in the instrument cabinet, and I saw the looks on their faces. They looked at one another and shook their heads. I knew the trouble I was in when my doctor patted me on the back as he walked past me. He immediately took a biopsy, but indicated that no matter which way the test came back, I would need a colostomy. I remember thinking to myself, "that's for old men!" I also knew I would get a second opinion. I did, and got the same answer. Here I was, sliding on the razor blade of life. All I needed was a blindfold and a cigarette.

I was flooded with the only emotion that I could have, evil's greatest tool, fear. I couldn't eat, sleep, or think. I did have one thought…when was the phone going to ring to give the message of the biopsy? When it came, I wasn't surprised. I was informed that I had malignant cancer and that I would have to go in for surgery the next day, Christmas Eve. At that time, I was also ending a long-term relationship, which further complicated my thinking and had also started me drinking. It was a four-month span of total depression, and I was still not out of the woods. I think the reason it took me so long to get a grip was that while I was on all the different medications, morphine, perks, and valium, I felt like I had to reach up to tie my shoe strings. My head wasn't clear enough to think straight. Thankfully, my buddy Sandy Christopher weaned me from the pharmaceutical amusement park.

The day after I threw a full bottle of valium down the garbage disposal, I engaged in a conversation with my brain, asking my brain pharmacy to start producing whatever chemicals it would take to get me right. I started with a new drink—the drink of the three wisemen (water), eight to twelve glasses a day. I gave myself a big-time carotene boost in the form of fresh, raw carrots that I got wholesale in fifty-pound bags at the produce market. From my Italian stallion buddy, Senator Ted Katalano, I also got ginseng, garlic, and raw beets and whipped them all up together in my Oster blender (a concoction I referred to as a "Lazarus Elixir Cocktail"). I found this concoction in a cancer newsletter, so I loaded myself up with this health elixir and with vitamins so my brain pharmacy would have the correct raw ingredients to put me back together.

Then I added the final ingredient, getting my sense of humor back. (For God's sake, I'm a comic and I'm doing tragedy.) I started dosing myself with two or three movies on video a day, all humor. Suddenly, there was a blood count turnaround in my body, and I knew that the most powerful ingredient in me was the humor. It was Groucho Marx who said, "laughter is like aspirin, only twice as fast." You see, schmoozing yourself to good health is just that. You can get help from the outside, but you need to start by getting help from the inside.

We make a lot of mistakes while we are healthy. We throw caution to the wind. Why? Because we pay $400 a month for health insurance in case we get sick. We don't know when that might be, but we'll spend it when we get sick. Well hey, how about *not getting sick?* How about taking some time out to water your inner flower?

You don't need to be a dietitian, a doctor, or even a genius to figure out that you simply need to take care of yourself better. Schmooze yourself to wellness before you get sick. As my mother use to say, "If you go sixty miles per hour when you're twenty, you'll go twenty miles per hour when you're sixty." You need to feed yourself better. You also know that you must exercise. And getting away from some of the chemically-induced meat and produce we gorge ourselves on would help too. Finally, and most importantly, find time for proactive inner thinking and good literature to feed your brain—don't be afraid to call upon the pharmacy of your brain to put the right chemicals through your body.

PROACTIVE PERSONAL TRAINERS

Going back to the year 3000 B.C., there were personal trainers who trained people to stay healthy. The Emperor would get the top dog in this business to keep him well, teach him when to do breathing exercises, water his inner flower, and, of course, exercise. The trainer's job was to never let the Emperor get sick. If the Emperor got sick, the trainer could get really sick—like dead-type sick.

Today, you need your own proactive inner thinking trainer. Let me give you an example. After my colostomy, my doctor told me, "Within six months, you will know the most about this colostomy...as you have one, and I don't." He then asked if at that time I would be willing to become a guide for other new colostomies. My answer was yes, as I had a great guide myself. (Thank you Vince Ingrelli, who owns VIP Plumbing. Take a look, only I would get a plumber to advise me on my colostomy—you just can't make this stuff up!)

So I found myself giving advice to other colostomies. I first got a young man who was twenty-eight years old and owned over a million dollars worth of eighteen-wheelers in his business. Along with his business came the responsibility and the stress. It was not a surprise to find out that he had an ulcerated stomach. The prize wasn't worth the pressure. The lesson? If you are in a job that you absolutely hate and you're making yourself sick, get rid of it. Lose it, or it's going to put a hurt on you.

One of the calls I received to aid with a new colostomy was from a lovely Spanish woman named Naomi. We knew from the start that we would probably never meet. We were merely consoling voices over the phone. But sometimes the conversations would go far beyond just talking about the common problem of how to keep your appliance clean. On this particular occasion, Naomi informed me that the experience was becoming quite difficult for her. It was causing trouble in her marriage. When she told me what her trouble was, I was slightly amused.

She explained that she was fifty-two years old and had eight children. Now that she had a colostomy, she thought for sure that her husband would no longer want sex from her. She felt ashamed because she had to wear an appliance on her side, but he never faltered. He continued wanting her, and she didn't know how to handle it.

Ironic as it was, at the very same time, I was dealing with a woman named Sue who had quite the opposite problem. She had just had a colostomy, and not only did her husband *not* want her, but he had moved into the other bedroom. I said to her, "would you mind if we shared your problem with someone else?" She agreed, as did Naomi. I made it a three-way conference call, and I told Naomi to tell Sue about her sex maniac of a husband. At the end, Sue laughed and said, "can you please send your husband to me?" And then Sue began to tell Naomi how her husband had moved out of her bedroom and no longer loved her. At that point, there was no point for me to be in on this phone conversation anymore. I felt as useless as a one-legged man at an ass-kicking contest. They exchanged numbers and talked some more.

The next day, I got a call from Naomi again. This time Naomi only spoke of how wrong she had been and how lucky she was to have the support and love from her husband. She recommitted herself to being a good wife. I don't know what Sue told Naomi, but I know that Naomi's husband owes Sue a lot of thanks.

I still talk to Naomi from time to time. She is now a bilingual instructor for new colostomies. As for Sue, well, we lost her recently to the cancer that was killing her and to the love that she didn't have for support. But at least for a time, she had me and Naomi for support. We were each others' personal trainers. As for me, when I was diagnosed, I was given a 60/40 chance of making it, with the 60 being the bad side. But I remembered that there have been hundreds of thousands of miracle cases where people have far outlived the death sentence doctors had given them. Keep that in mind when you need to create your own miracle.

For you, my recommendation to schmoozing yourself to health is to first get all the hate and unforgiven hurts out of your way, because you are on the way to getting well. Second, stay close to your support group. They are and will be important for your recovery. Keep working, it's important you have a goal. Think of watering your inner flower, and get a second opinion. Most importantly, get humor back in your life.

Finally, I'll give you one more tip, so when you have something traumatic to get through or overcome, you can get it all over with. Go someplace where you are absolutely in solitude, where no one can hear you. Yell, curse, and scream. Do all the "why me's" you can at the highest pitch of your voice and with all the anger you can muster. You can swear, curse, or yell at God if you like. Get it done all at one time, and be done with it. Then you can get on with the proactive inner thinking and keep with it. Make it like your virginity—you only get to lose it once. Then get busy living, and die young at an old age.

P.S. Yesterday I had my twelfth-year-in-remission checkup. Dr. Iglar said, "Whatever you're eating, keep on eating it," and I felt like it was a great day to be alive.

CHAPTER EIGHTEEN

OOZING SCHMOOZE ON YOURSELF

Proactive Inner Thinking

Iknew I'd need a sign from God, but I never dreamed it would come from the cover of *Life* magazine. In bold print, the headline read: "The Revolution of Mixing Ancient Medicines and the New Science to Treat Everything from the Common Cold to Heart Disease." It was imprinted over the torso of a young woman's body with one hand of a doctor on a stethoscope over her heart and the other handing her ancient prescription herbs. During the same week, three major news networks and three major TV news magazines made mention of what they called "white light healing." That's when I made the decision to share this with you.

WHITE LIGHT HEALING

I'm in love with proactive inner thinking even though I'm a late bloomer to the topic. I stopped using unproductive inner thinking, because I found that I was both living and dwelling in the past. But the past is only a lesson, not a lodging. It is also a never-ending science inside your head. What I'm about to express, I've learned the old-fashioned way—the hard way. I believe it to be as essential as the sun coming up tomorrow. If just one paragraph hits home with you, you just made my life. I'm not a preacher, and I'm not a teacher. I've just been there, done that, got my passport punched. It took a near-death wake-up call to make me realize it all. So please forgive me for these efforts at profoundness, and let me share with you what I finally figured out.

To be a schmoozer, you must first be proactive. That's the easy part. I believe that dysfunctional families are becoming a bit of a crutch in today's society. It has become too many people's reason that they're over-weight, drink, commit crimes, or do drugs. In fact, what's wrong is that their brain needs some self-schmoozing. When you stop asking yourself and start directing yourself, you're there, that's it! You are now proactive inner thinking, and it's not easy, but you can reach it. Take charge of your life. You will have a power you've never had before. Anything you wish to do with this energy that is being directed from your proactive inner thinking is now obtainable. You are no longer asking your brain, you have now become one with your brain. You are the new captain central. Focus on dictating your body to health and your mind to betterment. Did you get it? If you did, you are experiencing your first fresh feelings of enlightenment.

I think I'm too hyper to meditate, although I've been told that is what I've actually been doing, and I'm okay with that. The very first ingredi-ent you need is solitude, whether you find that in the bathroom or in the confines of your car. If you travel and you stay at a lot of hotels, these are also good places. You will soon learn that proactive inner thinking actu-ally is a journey into one's self. You are probably doing it already in the form of talking to yourself, whether it be silent or out loud. Out loud is okay—you'll never get an argument.

Try the following process to see if you can get to that peaceful place. Stop and sit back in your chair. Get comfortable and close your eyes. You may wish to put music that is soothing to you softly in the background. What you're trying to do is create a white light curtain in your mind and get rid of the junk in your attic. It's like a blossom releasing useless thoughts. You are running old demons that have haunted you for years sideways into a white light curtain, and once you've sent them through, they disintegrate into meaningless, nothingness, opening brain cells that were once held captive by their hateful hosts' presence. You can even feel your brain inside your skull opening up with a feeling of control, more loving and confident. By flooding your mind with white light, don't be afraid if you hit pay dirt, and cry or laugh till you're weak. Either one is good.

The multitude of miracles of proactive inner thinking renewed my life to a high gear of control. Twenty-some years ago, when I was in the middle of a very bad kidney infection, a young lady with extreme powers put her hands over my chronically aching middle-back. My first feeling was that she was pulling the hairs out of my back. Then I realized that she wasn't even touching me. I've never had that pain again.

I swear that what I'm about to share with you is true, though I'm the only witness. Being behind all the carnie games on the midway, knowing how most magic illusions are done, the gaffs and the gimmicks, the scams and shams, you've got to imagine that I'm a hard sell. Three things stick in my mind as real. Facing death six times, watching the birth and cutting the cords of my babies, and this life-changing story I'm about to tell you.

When I was released from the hospital after my cancer operation, I was staying with a friend of mine. I remembered the young woman who healed my lower back and what she had told me of her tool of the white light. When she drew whatever was wrong with my back into her hands, she glared at her hands and immersed them in white light to purify them. She told me she does it to herself all the time. Hey, it sounded strange to me, but what did I have to lose, besides cancer!

My buddy John "Gatsby" Iverson had taken me in when I got out of the hospital after the cancer surgery. I had just weaned myself off the pharmaceutical merry-go-round and anything else I was drinking, inhaling, or snorting at the time. I was wasting away, waiting to die. When I finally got a grip through friends, a healthy diet, and humor, alone one spring day, I remembered the Shaman-like young lady who fixed my lower back pains forever. It was the first time I had ever heard of the white light, but I thought, why not give it a whirl! I put on some Mozart very quietly, jumped into Gatsby's recliner facing the lake, closed my eyes, and tried to load off some worthless baggage. I thought first of anybody I disliked, making an effort to get rid of them by forgiving them. Then I began to forgive myself for all my dastardly deeds. I tried not to dwell, instead just admitting I was guilty for my sins and indiscretions.

Next, I wanted to try my own white light bath. It was hard at first. I tried to imagine different forms of light, like the arc from a welding torch, a flare, fireworks...nothing worked. I opened my eyes and looked out the window at the sun reflecting on the rippling water. Suddenly, I felt faint. I closed my eyes, and the light kept coming. For an instant, I was afraid, and I wanted to move and stop the sensation. For a moment, I thought I was really dying. But I remember thinking to myself, "I don't care," and I felt myself filling with a loving light. I quickly lost the feeling that I wasn't worthy, and I felt myself receiving as well as sending the greatest emotion of love I've ever felt. It was like I was overfilling with this light. Like it was shining out of my eyelids, my ears, nostrils, and every other orifice. I remember thinking that I would have loved to see the smile on my face. Concepts, ideas, and purposes were clear to me— talk about mixing business with pleasure.

It ended like it started—fast. It left me with no idea of how long I had been there. I bellowed with laughter, and tears poured out of me. I was emotionally wiped out. I kept saying, "Alright, alright, I'm going to be alright. Whatever happens to me, I'm going to be alright." I couldn't wait for Annie to come over so I could share it with her. At that moment, I knew I would marry her, we would have kids, and that she was my life-mate. I started writing this book that day. I knew that schmoozing was the only thing this ex-low life had to share.

What did the experience teach me? It taught me to make it from the first five minutes of life to the last five minutes of life. Make your mistakes, take your whacks, try not to hurt anybody on the way (though you will), and nobody's worth carrying their hate inside of you. Trite? Right! Did I ever do it again? No! Why? Answer: Been there, did it, got it. Do I still screw up? Did Abraham get shot in the temple?

As for the young Shaman-like woman, the white light mentor, she went on healing people for free, supporting herself by healing major league baseball and football players and jocks of all kind who paid her well. Then suddenly, she just dropped out, and I never heard from her again until just three months ago when I received a book she had written with a note inside. The note said, "All I have are fond memories of you and thought I would send you this and share with you what I've been doing for the last two decades." She had suffered a very dramatic near-death experience, and when she came out of it she wrote this wonderful book called *Verbal Elixirs*. It's little verses. I keep it on my desk, and once a day, I cleave into the book with my letter opener and randomly pick one of the verses to see how it refers to me. Today's verse was "Take sexual energy, raise it to mind level (love). It increases creativity." It's like she's talking to me! For the last three years, she has done a weekly radio show from Hawaii on self-health wealth. I believe she is the genuine article. You can hear the emotion in her voice on her thought tool tapes, the "I'm not here for profit" pure wisdom, with a touch of special insight knowledge. This book is the nearest thing I can think of to proactive thinking. I was already finished with my book when I next heard from her. The coincidence was right out of the twilight zone, or I wouldn't go through the trouble of recommending her book and enclosing her mailing address. Check it out: Yvonne Vunk Nielsen, P.O. Box 1717, Kailua, Hawaii 96734 (books $16.95 +$3.50 handling, Hawaii residents add 4% tax, Make check payable to Verbal Elixirs).

SELF-CLEANSING

Cleansing your inner self and losing all the baggage allows you to purify your memory bank. All hate, envy, jealousy, and bigotry has got to be dumped before you can even start to attempt the biggest clean out—self forgiveness.

Here is the schmooze exercise you will need to try. To begin your proactive inner thinking, start in solitude looking in the mirror and introducing yourself to yourself so that you can become yourself (get that?). You will find that it is a very awkward, yet very powerful thing to do. As you look into your eyes, see your inner soul and reunite with yourself. You should probably start the conversation by saying, "I do love you." This statement is very important and, I believe, very healthy. I truly believe that until you love yourself, you cannot love anyone else. Go on from there in your conversation and elaborate—you have a lot to talk over. Forgive yourself for every time you were a shit-heel, and thank yourself for every time you caught a break and gave one. By thanking yourself for what you have, at the very same time, I believe you are thanking your God and everybody standing on that ladder of your DNA.

It is clear that worldwide, mothers and fathers have to start teaching their children to love their bodies while they're young. They must be taught that they are one with their brain and can appreciate their health and their bodies. If this were done, humankind would so love the regular functioning of the body, that there is no way we would feel that we have the right to destroy our bodies with alcohol, drugs, and tobacco, or to kill other humans and the environment in which we live.

As you've read that sentence, take a guess at how many centuries after you're dead this type of world will ever come to pass. Be optimistic, and try not to say never. Try to think that some advanced civilization will figure a way to teach self-esteem in schools of the future.

CHAPTER NINETEEN

RELATIONSHIPS ARE EVERYTHING

We're All in This Together

Wisconsin can have harsh winters (we even get up to zero degrees once in a while) with lots of snow and freezing temperatures. (In fact, we define "relative humidity" as your wife's family working up a sweat digging you out of a snow bank.) As you might imagine, service stations and snow plow services are a hot commodity and can easily get backed up during big storms. One winter after a storm, I was at a service station when an older woman called to see if they could come plow her driveway. The attendant looked at the long list, and instead of putting her at the bottom of the list, put her at the top. I looked at him funny, and he said, "I'll plow her driveway first. That nice little old lady always gives me a piece of hot home-baked pasty!" He even went to the coffee machine to get coffee to go with the pasty he was certain would be waiting for him when he finished the job. What does that little old lady schmoozer know that you don't know? She knows who it's important to schmooze.

SCHMOOZING IN THE TRENCHES

Those people who work for "the people" (you and I) are some of the most important people you will ever encounter. They are the souls who work the trenches, and you may be one of them. If you are, then you know how important it is to be treated with respect for the work you do.

It's been said that if you want to measure your importance, stick your hand in a pail of water—the hole you leave when you remove your hand will be the measurement. Unfortunately, most "civilized" societies don't understand this adage, because we treat each other differently based on status, position, wealth, confidence, and appearance. How else could a movie star or sports figure pay to fly coach, yet ride first class? Why else would those people perceived as "important" get the best service at restaurants? But luckily, any class system can be countered through random acts of kindness and simple acts of schmoozing.

The supreme rule for schmoozing workers in the trenches is to let them know how important they are to you by giving them verbal bouquets, as well as gifts they can appreciate and use. For example, the most simple sign of respect is calling someone by their name rather than by their job description. But when was the last time you did so? In my case, anytime I sit down in a restaurant, I make sure to say to the waiter or waitress, "Hi good-looking, how are you? What's your name?" If they give me their name as a part of their greeting, then I tell them mine. "Hi, I'm Aye Jaye, and I will be your loyal patron for this evening." Rather than call them "waiter" or "waitress," I always refer to them as if they were a friend of mine. When I call the server back I'll say, "Excuse me Theresa, could you help me with this?" It's certainly a lot more respectful and pleasant than saying, "Hey, you!" or "Waitress."

The same rules apply when you are making a call to any business or store. The exchange, when you ask, "Who am I speaking with?" changes the tone of the conversation. (Always write their name down when they give it to you—you'll be surprised at how often you will need it again.) Again, when they give their name, say, "Hello, Russ, this is Muriel." The person on the other end of the phone knows immediately that they are not being treated like a number or a nuisance, and they are more likely to help you get what you need in an efficient and timely manner. Why? Because you have been introduced and have begun the bonding process.

Anywhere you go, try to develop a relationship with whomever you encounter, no matter if you think it will be a one-time encounter or not. Sometimes those one-time encounters can turn into longer ones. For example, in October, I took my snow blower in to be serviced, since I knew that if it broke in the winter, I'd be waiting until spring to get it back. Buzz, the kid who serviced it, found a mouse's nest in it and cleared it out for me. I paid the bill, but then I went back to find Buzz. I gave him five dollars and told him to go get a pizza with it. With that small act, I would remember him, and he would remember me. And I made a mental note (by seeing a buzz saw in my mind) not to forget his name.

Well, lo and behold, during the winter, my snow blower broke in the middle of the biggest storm on (of course) the repair shop's busiest day. Nonetheless, I took it in to be fixed. There were snowmobiles and snow blowers all over the yard waiting to be repaired, but the moment Buzz saw me pulling in, he walked up to me and asked what the problem was. I greeted him with, "Buzz my man, help me, help me." I'm sure he was impressed that I remembered his name. He looked at the snow blower, discovered the problem was a dirty gas filter, and he serviced it right on the trailer—and for no charge. This time, I left and came back with a pizza for him. Had I been a stranger to Buzz, this "one-time" encounter may have remained so. But because I had taken the time, energy, and thought to appreciate him, he took the time to help me when I needed it the most. It wasn't the five dollar pizza that was important, it was the thought that he counted and that we had connected.

Gilbert Gottfried and the Ice Cream Man

Developing relationships with the people in the trenches has its intrinsic and extrinsic rewards. Here's an example: The famous comic Gilbert Gottfried (and the voice of the parrot, Iago, in Disney's *Aladdin*) was performing at the Comedy Stage during a twelve-day run of Milwaukee's Summerfest. I was his opening act. At the end of the first evening, the two of us walked over to the ice cream booth to get a cone. It had closed fifteen minutes earlier, and the owner said, "come back tomorrow." Just our luck.

But the kids closing down the booth excitedly told the owner that the man with me was Gilbert Gottfried. Although he had no idea who Gilbert was, he saw how excited his crew was and invited us to the back door. The manager said to a beautiful crew worker, "give them anything they want." In less than a heartbeat, Gilbert replied, "if we can't have that, can we still have some ice cream?" The crew screamed with laughter. They may have been working during our show, but they had just gotten a personal appearance. By the boss recognizing his employees' reaction and allowing us in the back, he rewarded his crew for the hard day's work they had put in. The kids working the booth were thrilled to meet Gottfried, and he took the time to give his autograph to everyone who was working.

The owner of the ice cream stand invited us to come over every night, fifteen minutes after closing, to have a cone. He later told me it was the first time ever that no one missed a day for the whole run. In the following week, Gottfried's run had ended, but I was still performing, and even though he was the celebrity, I was still invited for a cone at the end of each evening (I even made up 31-Flavor jokes for my stage performance). It was because I had formed the relationship with the kids at the booth that I was able to go to the back door after hours and get ice cream. The kids would even begin to worry about me if I was late. And to reciprocate, I had juice (connections) at the carnival for ride tickets for the workers. I now buy all my ice cream at the owner's permanent store, and where do you think I tell people they *must* go for the best ice cream in town? Thus, a simple exchange such as this has turned into a long-term relationship.

HOME IS WHERE THE HEART IS

I had just signed a two-year lease on a coach house that was owned by a man who ran the apartment buildings next to it. He was the type of guy that, if you would cut him open, you would find a heart of the purest gold—but even if you didn't, it would still be worth it to cut him open. My fellow tenants had nothing good to say about the landlord; they warned me that the size of the landlord's heart was akin to a BB in a boxcar. Compared to him, Ebenezer Scrooge looked like a philanthropist.

Being duly warned, I figured that I had to schmooze him if I was going to enjoy my stay. I had recently won a croquet set at a raffle and I had no use for it, so I wrapped it up and sent it to my landlord. I attached a note of thanks and a few words about how this might be something he'd like, since he was such a family man, and how happy I was renting from him. The following month, I got new carpeting.

In the two years I lived in that building, the landlord never denied any of my requests, and he never raised my rent. I bet it was the first time anyone had ever laid anything on the landlord (anything but trouble, that is). Schmoozing people you don't have to schmooze may have surprising results.

Think for a moment about where your business takes you on a regular basis and who you should be schmoozing. For me, it's into the backstage areas of arenas, auditoriums, and convention centers. You can deal with the people who work there in one of two ways: you can demand what you want (but I guarantee that you won't get twenty-five percent of what you're looking for, not counting the sabotage you might encounter for making them angry), or you can schmooze.

Around arenas and convention centers, it's hard enough to find parking at all, let alone the days when you have to carry lots of heavy equipment. The goal, then, is to be at least in the proximity of the building so you don't get a hernia hauling your gear. Think of how nice it would be to know the guy who works at the shipping dock who can open those big, beautiful garage doors and let you drive in and leave your car. Pipe dream? Not if you know that his name is David Kiser and that he has eight kids. Oh, and you just happen to have ten extra circus tickets that you don't know what to do with. Would you give him the tickets?

You'll wish you had when the time comes for you to use this facility. Do this months before you need him. You are servicing the schmooze. And if you know you will be using the facility more than once or twice, it's a good idea, when you're in the neighborhood, to buy a dozen donuts and some coffee and just drop in and schmooze with David for ten minutes. I bet parking will be a breeze the next time you're looking for a space at the convention center. David will smile and open those garage doors because you took the time to think about him; you are no longer a stranger, but a friend. Relationships are everything!

If you park in the same place frequently, the same idea applies. It will only benefit you to start a relationship with the parking attendant. The majority of people who see the attendant every day will not even know his or her name. Once you start a conversation and find things that you have in common, it's easy to begin building a relationship. Find out about his hobbies, his collections, his health (and how is his Bull Terrier, Butkus?). Want to go nuts here? Find out his birthday. Bring some of *your* work mates and get a small cake with a candle. Now go down and make the parking guy's day—all of you sing Happy Birthday. Now he remembers *you all*, and you just taught your work mates to be better schmoozers. Soon, you may find that all of you are parked closer to the elevator or out of the snow or sun, and your car suddenly stops getting new dents. Basically, someone is watching out for you, and couldn't you use a few more allies?

SMALL TOWN RELATIONSHIPS

People today will commonly complain about how small town values and small town relationships have wasted away or been pushed aside. But in reality, the difference between a small town and a city can be mostly in your mind. That small town atmosphere is all about the way you feel about people and how you treat them.

Especially if you live in a large city, it helps to think in terms of starting a small town relationship with anyone who is important in your life. A plumber, a roofer, an electrician, a hairdresser, your beat cop, and even the employees who wash and wax your car at the local car wash—all are important people. If they are important to your life, be important to theirs. It's especially important to build relationships with those people whose services you are going to be using a lot. You don't have to ask them to do anything for free, although you will probably get better service because you have built a relationship with them. And why shouldn't you? You treat them nicely, you remember their name, and they like you. You have built a lasting relationship with them.

But in a busy city, availability is the key, and if you're a known, friendly entity, it is more likely that others will be available for you when you need them. Given the choice, they will be available for you before they will be available for a stranger or grouchy old man Schlebbuttnik. Wouldn't you want to help those you know and like first?

Here's another example: my van had a flat tire while I was driving on the expressway, and there was no way I could change it myself. On my car phone, I dialed the emergency number for help, and Bing, my operator, was very helpful. The wrecker and the state patrol came quickly to my rescue, and I was again on my way. The next day, I sent both Bing and Bing's supervisor a can of instant tire repair and a humorous note thanking them for their assistance.

Two weeks later, I won a second phone during a golf outing. But now I had two phones and only one line. I called my friend Bing. I asked if I had to buy another line for the second phone, and although he didn't have the answer for me, he gave me his full attention and said he would call me back with a solution. Later, he called back and said that they don't normally give out two different codes for one line, but *in my case,* they would make an exception since I had "a fleet of eighteen-wheelers." Funny—I don't remember having eighteen-wheelers. But it was nice to have two lines for an imaginary fleet. In essence, it's as if I had another line, but I only paid one bill. I had no idea that sending a humorous thank-you note would result in a favor from the phone company.

So the next time you're talking to that service person or that anonymous voice on the phone, think about how they've probably been treated all day, and give them a break. Give them a smile, a joke, heck, give 'em a piece of pie, because the next time you need a hand, you'll know who to call—and when you do, be sure to ask for Bing.

"Not one of us is as good as all of us."

—McDonald's Founder, Ray Kroc

CHAPTER TWENTY

SCHMOOZING FRIENDS AND NEIGHBORS

It's a Beautiful Day in the Neighborhood

L et's take first things first and talk about schmoozing the greatest people in the world: friends. Here's a wonderful toast that our group, the Life Trippers (code name: Bleacher Creatures) and I sing to one another:

Toast: Hey old friend.

What do you say old friend?

Here's to the bitter end.

Here's to us! Who's like us? Damn few.

The stock and trade of a true schmoozer is people. Why? Because if you're a schmoozer, you really do love them. You're a people person. You truly like them—you like to be around them, listen to them, look at them. You love to hear the voices of young kids, you sigh when you see young lovers, and you're romantic enough to look at an old face and try to remember when it was young. You love to watch people work and play.

OK, you might be reading this thinking, "no way, I don't like any of that." Well, if you are thinking that, that's probably why you're reading this kind of book in the first place. The truth of the matter is that if you're having a hard time liking other people, then you probably have a harder time getting along with them in the first place. My point is that if you can download some of that more positive, even romanticized thinking, life will automatically become easier for you.

I recently re-watched a wonderful movie with Hugh Grant, called *Four Weddings and a Funeral*—it's a real holler. I remember thinking the first time I saw it how lucky they were to have that wonderful, wacky support group. If nothing else, they had each other. The only measures you can use for your friends are their loyalty and their integrity. Someone once said that if you're lucky enough to have one good friend, you're very wealthy. I couldn't agree more. By this measure, I might be a billionaire, and all because I schmooze!

A GESTALT COMEDY TROUPE

Years ago, I was working with a comedy acting troupe who stayed together for a long time. It consisted of a dozen or more guys and gals. We were all very close, and we knew that we were each other's back-up system.

There was one person in the group who was very young and had a dishonesty problem. It was only because of his youth, but he knew he needed to come forward, get it out of his system, and get past it. At that time, he was carrying more baggage than Madonna on safari. He also had one of the worst cases of acne I'd ever seen in my life—he looked like the goalie for a dart team. Within one week (and this was witnessed by all of us), after we did a group gestalt (a German word describing letting all out) of coming clean on all matters, his skin was as clean and pure as a newborn babe. Coincidence? I doubt it. It is amazing how all of those brain cells were so busy holding in those untruths that it made his blood boil and come out in another way. How therapeutic to have people he trusted and loved with whom he could finally get all that behind him. The amazing thing is that today he is without a doubt one of the most honest persons I know.

Our group gestalt took place while we were touring and we had one afternoon off. We laid on the floor in one of our rooms, on our backs, head-to-head in a star shape, looking at the ceiling. One by one we revealed to one another our darkest fears and our innermost secrets, along with a pledge that for the rest of our lives we would be totally honest with one another and all of us would be forgiving. We also vowed that our integrity would be immeasurable, and we would be there for each other when needed.

It's twenty years later now, and though we have all moved on to different parts of the world, taken wives or husbands, and had kids, we stay in contact at least every two weeks via phone or mail. It has also come to pass that our undying support for each other has remained. When one of us faltered and had a fatal attraction with drugs and the dishonesty that comes with that disease, we were there and put him back on his feet. When another of us nearly died, all the rest were at that person's side, there to support him with whatever it took. I cannot think of any people on the earth that I love more than this group.

It's amazing how like a family we are—no, we are better than most families. We watch out for each other's kids like they're our own. God forbid, if something happened to a set of parents in our group, all properties and kids would go to someone from among our group (and doesn't that scare the hell out of you Carl and Punz?). In addition, we're always cognizant of birthdays, anniversaries, and special days (except for one of us who is graciously-impaired, but we all understand his pig-rudeness and forgive the bottom-feeding slug). And as you can imagine, anytime we can get a gag going just to keep some hub-bub in the group, we do it.

The ongoing prank for about ten years now is the swapping of a truly awful painting. I don't even remember which one of us originally picked it up. It's a painting that you must keep until you can finally get rid of it by laying it off on one of the others, but it has to be done cleverly. It's like receiving the Ebola virus, but it's more fun than you can imagine. It has happened even when one of us is at an affair that has nothing to do with our group. Somehow, the evil bearer of this hideous painting plans, infiltrates the event, and manages to present another with this awful gift. Find something ugly, and try it with your friends!

We have even figured out how to see one another every year. Most of us are in the business of show, and we all belong to the biggest kids' charity in the world, the heart of show business, Variety Club International. You don't have to be in the business to be a member, but you do have to work on the charity. There's generally a Variety Club tent in every major city in the free world. Here's the perk, though. Every year, we all get to meet in a different place in the world because we all go to work a major national event. And the price is right, because most tents furnish charters to the convention for its workers. The charity events are black tie and gowns, fish and soup, complete with stars, royalty, sports figures, comics, and theater owners. Our group also likes to get together and do New York for Thanksgiving. We all chip in and get one large suite and stay in it together. We party, do shows, watch the parade, see if we can get stage time at one of the comedy clubs, and do the football pool. Truly this group is my family. In my hometown, I only have one friend—new friends pour through a revolving door. The true test is the friends that have been there, ready to keep your heart pumping and stand you up if you should fall. You can't count their worth in gold. Treat them like that, because they really are rare and precious.

So, when schmoozing your friends, make sure you take the time out to state how important they are to you. If you have a great friendship, don't let it go unsaid. Tell the person how much you appreciate it so you can truly be a full part of that special person's life.

HARD SCHMOOZE LOVE

I feel I have to broach the subject of friends, trouble, and tough love. In dangerous times, tough love can at least save yourself, even if you can't save your friend. Somewhere among your friends or family perhaps you know someone who's in trouble or is constantly causing trouble for themselves and sometimes for you.

I pitch a two strike game. Two strikes and you're out. If you do me once, shame on you. If you do me twice, shame on me. I have always regretted giving a third strike. Here's a clue: if it looks like a quack, if it walks like a quack, if it sounds like a quack, it's a quack.

A parole officer friend of mine once told me (and if you say I said it I'll deny it) that if a perpetrator commits a crime, let's say it's rape, and is found guilty in a court of law, serves his time, and commits another rape, he should be put to death. That is his specialty crime, and he'll commit it again and again. Although many won't agree with her idea for punishment, the pattern is a fact. She sees this type of repeat behavior all the time, from burglary, dopers, dealers, grand theft auto, and right down the line. If they're repeat offenders of the same crime, then that's what they do—two strikes is the clue.

The reason I use her example is that when you get done by a friend, you sometimes have to bail out of the relationship. When you have a friend who thinks the seven deadly sins are a recommendation, and not a warning, bail out fast. When you have a friend who has a $200 a day cocaine habit, heroine addiction, drinking, or gambling jones, it might be time to bail out of the relationship. People with these problems spend their days lying, both to you and to themselves. Hard love dictates that if they don't accept rehab, get away with your heart, life, and your VCR. That's called the Hard Schmooze Love.

HELLO, NEIGHBOR

Now on to neighbors. Well, if you can have a good friend who lives next door, then that's the best of both worlds. The old saying goes that good fences make good neighbors. I choose not to believe that, because there is nothing better than a chat with a good neighbor. Of course, having good neighbors is having good friends. Make sure that they're a part of your family and that you're watching out for their family, their property, *and their privacy.*

Good neighbors can also save you a lot of time and trouble. You would probably be surprised to know the skills your neighbors have and how willing they might be to put those skills to work with you. By the same token, you surely have some talent, hobby, or profession that might help out a neighbor, even if it's just a material thing. For example, one of my neighbors and I have a deal where I will always snow plow his driveway, which gives me free reign of his aluminum ladder. It's a simple arrangement that makes things a little easier for both of us. You see, when they first moved in, my wife was the first one to not only call the Welcome Wagon, but also to follow them in with her own basket of goodies. Two hours later, they were still chatting and forming the foundation of a good neighborly relationship. Our new neighbors knew if they needed us for anything, they shouldn't be afraid to call.

Similarly, if there's an old person or a shut-in in your neighborhood, make it your duty either by yourself or as a neighborhood group to watch out for this person. Here are three reasons: first, aging is your own inevitable fate; second, what goes around, comes around; and third, though it should not be your main reason, I know of three people who have been left heirs in people's wills because of their caring.

I was once totally blindsided to discover that I was made heir to the wonderful property I live on today. And the reason is simple, yet it meant a lot. You see, when I cook, I can't make small portions. I use my mom's giant old kettle, meaning I always had way too many leftovers. Luckily, I discovered an old man down the road who fixes things. One day when he was sharpening my saw, I noticed he was cooking shrimp subgum. When I looked further, I found his house was filled with cans of the stuff. He had bought the whole lot of shrimp cans for five cents on the dollar.

It was frugal, but not much of a daily diet. Eureka! I found a place for my leftovers. So for seven years, I cooked my heart out without guilt of throwing any of my leftovers away. Plus, I loved talking with Nick. He was funny, smart, cunning, and a shrewd business man, plus a compulsive schmoozer. So the day his executor told me Nick had left me the place for just a small remaining tax bill, I was floored and flattered. Nick had schmoozed me back in the most incredible of possible ways.

With your neighbors, don't let petty things get in your way, like a branch overhanging on your neighbor's property. Be the first to volunteer to cut it off if it's bothering them. Make any concession you can live with. If you see that a tree has fallen in their yard, be the first one to go over and help in any way you can. If any physical project is going on at your neighbor's home, offer to help, especially if they are elderly or in no shape to be doing heavy work. In fact, get a group together and put the yard in shape for them. You must acquire the attitude that you're all in it together. After all, nothing will make your property less valuable than horrid neighbors. And if you have a quibble with your neighbors, try to mend that fence any way you can, even if it takes an extraordinary effort to come to a friendly coexistence. If you can't do it alone, ask a third-party (someone close to them) to act as an ombudsmen to patch the fence. Last item on mending with neighbors: even if you don't get along, always do neighborhood watch. It's your duty both as a human and as a citizen. And who knows, you could someday save the day, and that would bring you back together.

So, on Christmas Eve (or whatever holiday is great for you on the spur the moment) remember to tip-toe over and leave a surprise at their back door with a card stating how great they are as neighbors. When you have an abundance of anything that grows in your garden, place it on their porch with a great neighbor note. Do random acts of kindness. They will be long remembered. After all, when you choose not to schmooze your friends and neighbors, your alternatives are simple: either you pay a lot of money for a shrink, or you get some good friends you can vent to.

CHAPTER TWENTY-ONE

THE TRICKY SCHMICKY SCHMOOZE

Half Schmooze, Half Trick (I Call It "Schmick")

You are privy to this chapter because, for reading this, I hereby deem you a schmoozer, which now entitles you to become the new magic-buying public. Have you ever had to present an idea? Advertising agencies have to do it all the time to pitch the client, which is why I'm about to give my fifth "schmick" seminar to the graduating class of one of the best colleges in America, Northwestern University, in Evanston, Illinois. It is taught by the Senior Executive of Marketing and Advertising of McDonald's, Professor Roy T. Bergold. He informs me that schmick is one of the most important parts of making a presentation. He says, "Schmick is going to be the point-after of getting you the account. The levity, bells, knobs, and whistles given to the top-spin to your obvious *knowledge and understanding* of their product will bring the account home every time. If they feel you know the territory, and that they can like you and live with you, they will pick you. I have witnessed hundreds of times that the presenters with the most schmick get the golden rings and go to Disneyland every time."

So, if you're dealing in sales with buyers, committees, or boards, you cannot afford not to pick up on this recommended schmick I have gathered for you in the form of books, tapes, and videos. These are absolute treasures with volumes of information that will make you a top-notch "schmickster."

The Tricky Schmooze can be the most fun of all. I have known people who have become rich and successful by using this type of schmooze. For example, schmickster Barry Lubin is a salesman I know who can do one hundred different sleight-of-hand magic tricks with the simple items on a customer's desk. Steve Nubie's schmick is one hundred different things you can do with a matchbook. Eric Clark is a very successful schmick lawyer in Detroit who buys balloons that he shapes into animals for the bailiffs, secretaries, and anyone else who passes his way in the courthouse. Once, when a baby was crying in court, he asked the judge for a thirty-second recess while he twisted up a very fancy poodle balloon and gave it to the child. The child stopped crying, and the judge said, "Thank you." Incidentally, Eric won that case.

THE MITT-CAMP WATCH DODGE

Schmick can be done either single-handedly or with the aid of a confederate. A confederate can be anybody you deal with a lot. Now, we are not talking about *sim-salabim* sleight of hand or presto/change-o magic here. We are talking about something very easy and lots of fun to do.

Here's an example I've used before. In fact, it's this very trick that is featured in the section on me in the book *Penn & Teller's How to Play in Traffic*. (If you love this chapter, you *must* buy Penn & Teller's book today.)

Here's how the ruse goes. You take people such as a client or a group of clients to a restaurant, preferably one that the others will know you are not familiar with. You notice somebody wearing one of those great watches with the stem on it, and you ask to borrow the watch. Then, you take a table napkin, put the watch on top of the napkin, and tell the client to pick out a waitress. When the waitress comes over, you pick up all four corners of the napkin and hand it to her. Next, ask her to take the napkin into the kitchen and reset the watch to another time.

When she leaves, take out your pen and write on a piece of paper the prediction of the time to which you think she will set the watch. Turn the paper upside down, and put a salt shaker on top of it. The waitress will return from the kitchen and produce the napkin with the reset watch in it. When you open it up, the watch will say 6:33. Then you reveal your prediction by taking the piece of paper from beneath the salt shaker and turning it over. Lo and behold, it too says 6:33.

Are we talking magic here or not? Absolutely not. The part of the trick the other person didn't get to see was *how* you put the watch inside the napkin, and the little note you dropped into that bundle. When you folded the napkin, you took up three corners, in one hand, and with the other hand, you placed the watch and the following note, which you had pre-written and palmed inside your hand: "Please keep the money and the note. Set the watch to 6:33, and thank you for joining in on the fun." Attached to the note is a two or five-dollar bill. You then quickly pulled the fourth corner up to the top, forming a little bundle. That's all there is to the trick, but just watch as your guests try to figure out how you did it. One thing is for sure—you will have made yourself memorable, both to your guests and to the restaurant.

THE GREAT SALOMONE, KING WIZARD OF THE MOLE PEOPLE

Here's another example of a fun schmick you can do for friends, colleagues, clients, or whoever. This one requires a confederate—a partner in crime—and it comes from the amazing Penn & Teller. Now, I would kill to see Penn & Teller any time I'm able. They are always new, always inventive, and I, like Penn & Teller, hate magic. But I love the tricks. And I *especially* enjoy card tricks that don't use cards.

For this trick, you will need an invisible deck of cards and a confederate you can depend on to be at a phone when necessary, or to play along at a moments notice. First, for your mark (guest/victim), produce an invisible deck of cards. Shuffle it, and ask your mark to please take a card. Then tell the person to put the card back in the invisible deck. You start to shuffle, and say, "Oops, you know, I forgot to look at the card. It doesn't matter. It's an invisible deck. What was the card you chose?" Let's say the mark said the eight of clubs.

Now, you go to the telephone, dial your confederate (whom you will now refer to as the Great Salomone King Wizard of the Mole People) and say, "May I speak to the Great Salomone King Wizard of the Mole People?" At this time, your confederate at the other end of the line has received your signal and starts counting, "1, 2, 3, 4, 5, 6, 7, 8" The confederate should continue counting until you interrupt in one of two ways. When you hear "eight," either say, "Yes, I would like to speak to the Great Salomone King Wizard of the Mole People," which indicates to him that he should stop on that number, which is the one the mark picked. Or, if you are using a touch-tone phone, push any one of the numbers (without letting the mark see, or under the guise that you are getting through a voice mail system). This will make a beep and stop the confederate from counting.

Your friend will then read off the card suits, "diamonds, spades, hearts, clubs," until you say, "Just a second," or push the touch-tone again at the right suit. The confederate now knows the card. Hand the phone to the mark, and tell the mark to say, "Hail, oh Great Salomone Wizard of the Mole People." Your confederate will answer (in the scariest of voices), "Your card is the eight of clubs—also, your great, great, great, great-grandfather says hello, and congratulations on—oh, wait. That's not until next week..." Then hang up.

This an especially fun thing to do for spouses, best pals, or even your kids, as long as you can depend on your Salomone King Wizard of the Mole People to be waiting for your call. Here are a few extra tips to make it run more smoothly: It is best is to have more than one wizard in case one's not home. If your confederate goes past the number because a signal is fouled up, be silent and your confederate should start the count over again. Your counting procedure and signal should be rehearsed ahead of time so you and your confederate will know what to do in case of a screw-up. Once you and a partner get it down, you can play this gag on countless people for the rest of your lives.

TABLE SCHMICK

Table schmick is a lot of fun and always livens up dinners and meetings. There are books on this subject, but here's one you may want to work out with a confederate ahead of time. The trick begins by having one person at the table hold a table napkin over your eyes, while another person at the table touches one of three items that you have placed in front of you, such as a salt shaker, a wine glass, and a sugar bowl. When the person has touched the object, you suggest that a physical imprint has been left on it that will throw off a vibration. Then, you take your hand and wave it over the objects one by one, until you begin waving it wildly over the object that the mark has selected, pretending you are picking up the vibrations from the object.

You can do this in a couple of ways. Have your confederate at the table take an object like a knife or a fork and place it either to the right, middle, or left of where they are sitting. The minute you look at that object on the table, wherever that person is sitting (hopefully in a strategic spot), you will be able to pick up on where the object is. The other way is to touch feet under the table. As you wave your hand over the correct object, your confederate will nudge your toe. It also can be done with your confederate having a toothpick sticking out of their mouth either to the left, right, or middle. For this trick, I thank my own confederate, Linda Kravitz, who often attends dinners and presentations with me.

Another fun one you might want to try with a confederate is taking a salt shaker, wrapping a napkin over it, and letting everybody at the table reach under the napkin to feel the salt shaker. The last person you let reach under the napkin is your confederate. Instead of feeling the salt shaker, your confederate will take it. Hold the napkin low enough over the table so that as the person "feels it" it drops into his or her hand. Then bring the napkin back in front of you, which will still hold its shape of the salt shaker. Put the napkin on the table and crush it with your hand. Of course, the salt shaker is gone.

Now, if you really want to have fun, take the empty napkin and go around to all the people again and have them feel under it again to prove nothing is there. The last person you have feel it will be the confederate, who this time will replace the salt shaker with a pepper shaker. When you bring the napkin back to crush it, this time you will crush it and show that something is under the napkin—the *pepper* shaker. As simple as this trick may sound, you will be amazed by the people who can't figure out that you are using a confederate to pull it off.

Here's another trick you can try: Get a silver dollar from the bank, and carry it in your pocket as a "lucky piece." Then go to the hardware store and buy a glass flashlight lens (they cost about 15 cents). The flashlight lens will be very close in size to the silver dollar. Now, take a Collins glass (tall and frosted) and fill it with water. No ice, just water. Produce the silver dollar, and at the same time, have the flashlight lens palmed in the center of your hand. (Don't worry, it's clear, so no one will see it.) Take the silver dollar and bang it on the side of the glass. Then ask somebody to cover both of your hands with a napkin. This will give you easy manipulation to take the flashlight lens, place it into both your hands, and palm the silver dollar.

Then, have your mark grab what appears to be the silver dollar through the table napkin. Take your hands out from underneath the napkin, and tell the mark to hold the supposed silver dollar in his or her hand. By now, you have had enough time to retrieve your hands to your lap and put the silver dollar underneath you so you can bring your hands back to the table.

Now, gesturing with your hands and fingers, say, "Tap the silver dollar on the inside of the glass and then imagine it disintegrating in your hand. Finally, let it fall into the glass." (They should leave the napkin draped over the glass.) When it falls into the glass ask them the question, "Did you hear it drop into the water?" Then ask, "Can you imagine it is gone? Now, remove the napkin." The circumference of the flashlight lens will completely take up the bottom of the glass. As the person looks into the glass, he or she will be able to see right through the bottom of the glass and, presto/change-o, the silver dollar is gone. Wow! You're a magician. And all it took was the right size props and a little sleight-of-hand.

Here is a prediction trick I like to do, and it can be done many different ways. You will understand the minute I explain it. Maybe you'll even be able to use it as an example for something you are trying to explain in a meeting. Here is how it works: You need three colored markers (red, blue, and yellow), a pencil, an envelope, and four pieces of paper.

On one piece of paper, draw a red circle. On the second piece of paper, draw a blue circle. On the third piece of paper, draw a yellow circle. On the back of the blue circle, write, "You will pick blue." On the pencil, write, "You will pick yellow." In the envelope, put the fourth piece of paper that says, "You will pick red."

Have your mark point to one of the three colored circles on the table. When your mark makes his or her selection, you will reveal that you knew what they would pick. For example, if they pick blue, turn over the papers with the red and yellow circles to show that nothing is written on the backs of either. Then turn over the blue circle, which will say, "You will pick blue."

If they pick yellow, pick up the blue circle and the red circle and put them aside. Ask the person to read what's on the side of the pencil (which has been lying anonymously on the table), on which you have already written, "You will pick yellow."

If the person picks red, collect the pencil, pick up the blue and yellow circles, and say, "Open the envelope." Inside will be the prediction card that says, "You will pick red."

You can make this trick on a bigger scale also, and you can specially tailor it for business or client presentations. On two-foot cardboard displays, put your client's product in three different colors. Then show them your ability to know which one the customer will buy.

When you show your tricks, you will also learn tricks from other people. Tricks are great ice-breakers. Remember at all times that if anybody asks you to redo a trick, tell them that the first time is magic, but the second time is education—at $500 a half hour.

MAGIC RESOURCES

We have just scratched the surface of the thousands of tricks you can do. But you probably only need a repertoire of a couple of them. Your local magic store will supply you with all the further tricks you need. Here's how magic stores work: If you walk in and say, "show me a trick," he'll show you a trick. If you say, "I like that," and put your money down, he will show you how to do the trick. If you don't say anything, he will simply put the trick back on the shelf and not show you how to do it.

The most expensive magic you will ever buy is magic you don't use. So take your time in selecting the tricks that are good for you. Keep it simple to start with. If you're just beginning, you're mostly looking for pocket magic—things that you can put in your pocket.

OK, let me open my schmick treasure chest and allow you to dig in to some of the best-kept secrets of sales schmick success. Here are some books and even a video for you to look at that will help you out. Some wonderful books to learn from are *Kid Biz*, by David Gen, *Mark Wilson's Course in Magic*, *Newspaper Magic*, by Anderson & Marshall, *Abbott's Encyclopedia of Rope Tricks for Magicians*, *The Buck Book*, and *Folding Money*.

Another one is *Magic for Dummies* by David Pogue with Mark Levy, from IDG Worldwide Publishing. And on video, first get *The Table Crape*, starring the worldwide dean of all magicians, Jay Marshall. If you are a salesperson, I especially recommend Marshall's video. Next, get *Tom Mullica's Expert Impromptu Magic Made Easy*, Volumes I, II, and III. All three are a must—if you can't find schmick here, you are schmick-impaired. I just love listening to this guy's style. He is the epitome of the genuine article and probably the greatest inventor of magic today (don't believe me, ask Copperfield). Kevin James *Rules of Thumb*, Volumes I, II, and II. Again, all three are a must. Last, but not least, *Max Maven's VideoMind*. There is a great prediction schmick here. Volumes I, II, and II are good for all occasions, and, of course, are a must. All of the above come with few or no props. They are truly a great value for your money and your library.

Visit your local magic store for any of these books, videos, and for tricks themselves. Any books or tricks that you will not be able to find there can be obtained through two large magic houses: Abbot's (124 St. Joseph, Coland, Michigan 49040; or call 1-800-92MAGIC—and tell 'em Aye Jaye sent you) and Magic Incorporated (5082 North Lincoln, Chicago, IL 60625; or call 773-334-2855).

Soon you'll be wowing nephews and nieces, dinner guests, clients, and everybody else who now knows you have a magic trick up your sleeve. Just remember, don't overdo it, or they'll want *you* to disappear.

Lastly, on page 175 is my magic handout when I teach a trick. You may want to copy this and use it at your presentations or seminars.

This is one of the best, cheapest giveaways in the world. You get people's attention at your gathering by having one of these rolled up, sitting in front of each participant. You explain to them, "pick up the wand in your left hand, put your right hand around your left wrist, raise your left thumb, your left pointer finger, middle, ring, and pinky fingers, one by one." All the magic wands will fall to the floor. Except yours. You then turn to face the audience exposing the pointer finger from your right hand is holding the wand in place. It will get a great laugh. Have them pick up their wands and go through it again, this time showing them how. Only this time, remove your pointer finger, and they will be amazed as yours stays in place because you have attached double-sided tape to your hand and the wand. This is known as a "blow off." Now inform them that if they remove the rubber bands and unfold the magic wand, there are instructions on the inside for how to do this trick, and space left over to put any important messages about you or your company beneath that.

If you need a magic tech for a creative or schmick seminar, I can be reached at:

Box UNIROK
Okauchee Lake, WI 53069

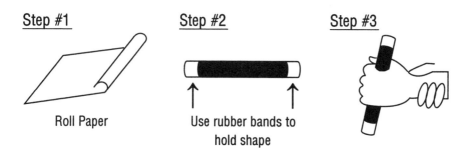

Step #1

Roll Paper

Step #2

Use rubber bands to
hold shape

Step #3

Step #4

Step #5

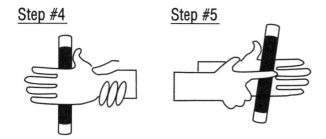

THE "BLOW OFF"

The best "chatch" (gifts) you can ever give will be non-material.

There is no way you can give without receiving—even if it is just a good feeling you get from the giving. Whether it be a compliment, a warm greeting, or one of the following tricks, you will have broken the ice and endeared yourself to a special new person, who won't be able to help but return the warmth they have just received. So try these games with children, friends, relatives, business clients, or anybody that you would like to engage with these wonderful, playful gifts.

Use stir sticks, straws, or whatever can be substituted for this brain teaser.

"4 + 5 = 9... right?" "I can make 4 + 5 = 10. Can you?"

"This one is a little harder...now, I have five squares of equal size. Can you move only two straws and make *four* squares of equal size?"

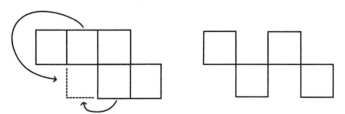

"Connect all the dots using only four straight lines—but, you cannot lift your pencil from the paper."

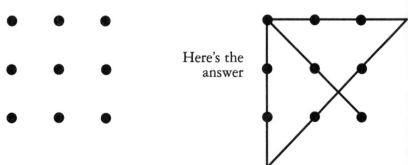

Here's the
answer

CHAPTER TWENTY-TWO

THE NAME SCHMOOZE

The Name of the Game

Here's the name game—memorize this little rhyme and fill in the blank with the name of a person to whom you've just been introduced:

"_____ is so very nice.

I always take her good advice.

She is soft and warm like bunny fur.

I sure do love her.

A poem for _____."

It also works if you use him (people won't be paying attention to the fact that it is not 100 percent on).

Whether it is at a convention, business meeting, or party, anytime I meet someone wearing a name tag, the words of the name game poem are my first. It always seems like you made up the poem on the spot just for that person. But please don't recite it a second time within earshot of the first person, and definitely don't overdo it at a small gathering. Or instead, use it as a throwaway gag when you're obvious—it's good for a laugh. Or, if you're in a reception line, say "You two are the best-looking people I've seen tonight" to the couple you are addressing, making sure you are within earshot of the people coming up. As soon as the first couple passes, say the same sentence to the next people. It will generate a laugh, and the couple who just passed will say "hey, you just said that to us." I reply, "what a coincidence, you people have to know one another," giving me the opportunity to introduce them. Then start it all over again. It's a great mixer.

NAME-DROPPING

Did you notice how throughout this book you have gotten to know the names of many of my friends, acquaintances, and business associates? Well, frankly, I've been name-dropping. Did you notice the size of my acknowledgments? Did I do it to schmooze these people? Well, yes, I did. But that wasn't the only reason. I also wanted to get you accustomed to this particular schmoozing technique. Any dinner or luncheon table at which you are seated with strangers, be the first one to introduce your companion and yourself. Then, have everyone else introduce themselves. As they go around the table, make up fantastic titles for each individual as they introduce themselves. For example, "We're Steve and Rhonda Jones," gains a reply of "Not the famous husband and wife astronaut team Steve and Rhonda Jones!" They generally laugh and say "yes." I live by the motto, "get a new laugh, get a new friend." Next, "not Todd and Stefanie, the great German archaeology team!" and on and on until your names and titles have everybody talking and getting on to having a great time. You've also created a memory chain to remember their names.

Now, if it's a business meeting table, draw a picture of your table on your notepad. Make X's to represent the chairs, then write your name at your X. Now, as they go around the table introducing themselves, write their name at their X. Then, when addressing them during your meeting, you can always use their first name (now that you have it so handy). Even if they think they know how you're remembering all their names, they will still be impressed that you took the time to do so.

You see, name-dropping has somehow become associated with stories about encounters with famous people. Well, I say we take name-dropping back for the average Joe. I say we've lost the art not only of remembering each other's names, but also of using other's names as often as possible. And the more unique your memory and use of someone's name is, the more memorable you become. Thus, the Name Schmooze.

I owe a lot to Tom Christopher. When I was overseas in Europe, he directed the play "Twelve Angry Men" on a tour of every military base in Europe. He had the good taste of picking me, out of hundreds of GIs he auditioned, to play juror seven in that cast (for which I am eternally grateful). Tom has recently won some Emmy Awards for his acting in daytime television. In his acceptance speech, he did what they all do—by name, he thanked everybody that was responsible for him being there on this great night. But right after he got off stage, he remembered he had forgotten to mention his wife!

He wanted to die, but he managed to atone. Every interview he did that night after the ceremony, from CNN to Japanese television, started with, "I'd like to first thank my wife, Judith, for being so understanding." Which she was. After all, whether you're accepting an award or making out a party list, forgetting the absolutely, positively, *most* obvious person is a faux pas that we all do from time to time.

It is impossible to overestimate how important using another's name is to the person listening. So, in either written or verbal form, when you get a chance to include the name of a colleague to show your unity and integrity, do it! Use their names as many times as you can in a single conversation. They more easily become kin to you, and there is a better chance of a special, honest, personal relationship coming out of it for the both of you. A great example of creating relationships through Name

Schmoozing is in one of my favorite films, *Being There*, starring the late Peter Sellers. Rent it, learn it, and share the warmth. His character, Chancey Gardener, is a real gardener, who uses proper names like a mantra (like "it's good to be with you, Glen," "Glen, I like your new idea," and "Let's do it immediately, Glen"). What is he doing here? It's almost hypnotic. It's music to your ears, that of the flute of a snake charmer. He's playing your song, and you feel T.O.M. (Top of Mind).

WHAT'S IN A NAME?

Now the first rule of Name Schmoozing is to get the name right. As soon as you're introduced to someone, think of somebody you know with the same name to help you remember the new person's name. It could be the name of a relative, a friend, a movie star, anybody—and if you've never heard the name before, rhyme it with something. Above all, don't forget the person's name. And if you do forget it, don't be afraid to ask a friend or colleague to help you out. In a pinch, turn your forgetfulness into a self-depreciating joke, and just flat-out ask for their name again (I tell them I have "Sometimers," a less advanced form of Alzheimer's).

True Name Schmoozers pay special attention to their notes—heck, no one can remember everyone. So if you're writing the name down in your note or address book, first and foremost, be sure you spell it correctly. If you picked up any special information in your conversation, include it in your address book, especially if you gleaned their birthday, the name of his or her spouse, children, pets, or whatever you're into, such as fishing, antiques, other hobbies, etc. Especially when it comes to business contacts, you need to also keep track of things you talked about (price, projects, jobs, etc.), things you found interesting about the person, or people or things you had in common. Keep this information handy, especially if you think this person's going to be along for the long run in either your work or personal life. If you don't, you may find yourself trapped in an embarrassing situation, or worse yet, in an embarrassingly forgetful dilemma.

You have probably noticed that most corporations today put a sign in the lobby welcoming guests by name to their company. Some hotels welcome the bride and groom on the marquee. It's the Name Schmooze. People love to see their names in lights! Did you ever notice during the Academy Awards that the winners thank many people you've never heard of—you're figuring, "who cares?" I'll tell you who cares—the people who have just been named. They care, and that's hot—even if it's just Mom and Dad in Pocatello. They heard it (and so did all their friends), and they're delighted.

In the business world, the Name Schmooze is truly the way to the top. Case in point, a CEO friend of mine, let's just call him Q, walked up to me and whispered, "What's the lady from marketing's name over there with the brown dress?" After receiving the name, the CEO walked right up to her and said, "How's it going, Mary Kay? Good to see you again," like the person was an old friend. Dishonest? Hardly. That was just plain smart (don't you wish you had done that instead of hiding in the corner avoiding eye contact?). It just goes to show you that the CEO realizes the importance of the Name Schmooze. What's in a name? A chance to schmooze.

NAME YOUR FAVORITE PERSON

I love doing Name Schmoozes. One of my favorites is always prepared if I have special guests coming over. For this Name Schmooze, I have placed a huge roll of white paper on the balcony over my garage that can be pulled down to the blacktop. I then write out a big welcome sign, personalized for our guests, and stretch it over the balcony. It never fails to be special for our guests, plus, I like to tell them that the sky divers who were going to spell out their name couldn't make it that day and the bus broke down for the high school band that was going to form the person's name on the lawn. I apologize and say the best I could do was the sign. Sound a bit overblown? Try it yourself, and I guarantee that if your friend has a camera, he or she will take a picture of the sign.

Recently, I was at a "rib and roast" for my friend Saz from Saz's Rib House and Bar. We're talking big success. Let me describe Saz. He is just a little teddy-bearish, always has a great boyishly friendly look on his face, and has a totally disarming personality. Oh, and he also seems to know the first name of everyone on the planet.

We all know the three most important factors in real estate site selection: location, location, and location. Here's an exception to that rule. For two years, Saz tended bar in a great location next to a sports arena. Whether you were a season ticket holder or maybe just went to a game or two a year, somewhere along the way, Saz would have waited on you, introduced himself, and asked your name. Without fail, the next time you came in, no matter how long it had been, he would call you by name, which is, of course, very impressive both to you and to anybody who is with you. He'd inquire if you were going to the game, if you had good seats, who you thought was going to win, and so forth. But inside your head and heart, Saz was your buddy, not just because he remembered you, but because he remembered your name.

Two years later, Saz took his talents sixty blocks west to open a joint in a barn-like building under a viaduct in an industrial area. He envisioned transforming it into a unique place, and because of his ability to make everyone he met feel special (not to mention because he had the best baby back ribs in town), he did. People drove out of their way to go to Saz's. Before games, they happily inconvenienced themselves by boarding buses just to go to his place. His Name Schmooze helped make him the single greatest promoter I've ever seen.

Lastly, remember that logos and mascots are often thought of as names, and a great, memorable gift is a flattering framed creation of their logo and mascot done as a collage, cartoon, or photo, with a brass plaque thanking them for doing business with you, with your name or your company's name at the bottom. Talk about staying T.O.M.!

CHAPTER TWENTY-THREE

WINNING BY GRINNING SCHMOOZE

Why Don'tcha Grin?

Y ou know what happens when a comic dies? All of his friends go up and say, "Hey, nice set." Because I wear my Pierrot heart on my sleeve, and it's the only dent in my armor, allow me to list the reasons I am including this chapter:

1. It's my nature to make people happy, be it by humor or deed

2. Scientists have proven that happiness leads to longevity

3. Or maybe it's because I read in the *New England Journal of Medicine* about Mr. Norman Cousins, at the time editor of the Saturday Review, who checked himself out of a hospital with a life-threatening disease and into a nice hotel (which was still cheaper than the hospital). He started watching videos of Candid Camera, Marx Brothers, Stooges, and Laurel and Hardy. He literally laughed himself into well-dom.

4. Or, how about because my heart goes out to people who, for one reason or another, carry on their no-humor, self-abusing lifestyles. I'm only guessing, but maybe it's because of cruel, over-religious, crazy, or unloving parents, the loss of a loved one, or they've stayed too long on the substance-go-round. Yet, I have brought people out of these

doldrums and into seeing life on the lighter side. So I know it can be done. Please help me, I'm only one.

In this world, there are more old drunks than old doctors. So when I see a funge (frown), I feel it my duty to turn it upside-down. Did you know clowns and comics live longer than most people? George Burns made it to one hundred. Red Skelton and Bob Hope into their nineties. Henny Youngman—stone-age. And the famous clowns Lou Jacobs, the Sherman Brothers, and Barry Lubin—all in their nineties. Does that tell you something? When you walk in as a performer, presenter, lecturer, or solo, you have less than ten seconds to make them like you. The most disarming tool that you have to wield is a real, warm, "I'm glad to be alive" smile.

Everyone has bad days; days where nothing seems to go according to plan. You've probably have had a few of your own. Try to recall one of those dismal days. Were you able to stop yourself from being abrupt, negative, or unpleasant to the people you met? Did you consciously try to do anything to counteract the gloom or doom you may have felt? Or did you just plow your way through the day, knocking over whatever and whomever was in sight, until you were finally able to shift your perspective and let go of your frustration or disappointment?

Recent research has shown that it's not the "hurry-up" attitude of Type A behavior, but the hostility that comes along for the ride, that wreaks havoc on the immune system. What that means is that you can charge around all day long, rushing to the beat of the band, as long as you don't become upset about it. The best way to not become hostile about events, especially the inevitable, unpredictable "turn of events" that you'll encounter somewhere along the road, is to maintain a good sense of humor. If you've ever had a sour mood turned completely around because someone or something made you laugh, then you know that humor can be a saving grace. It can save your relationships from ruin and your body from completely breaking down.

Enjoy the Merry-Go-Round Ride

I wholeheartedly believe in the old showbiz adage, "Always leave them laughing!" My main goal each day is to get a laugh or a least a smile within the first thirty seconds of an interaction with someone, but particularly from the person least likely to smile...the person in a hurry or a huff; the person who's grumpy, stiff, or gruff. Humor is such a powerful communication tool that even the most rigid of people will respond to it. Because it's nearly impossible to smile and be angry at the same time, they'll drop their defenses and their Star Trek deflector shields at the same moment. For that moment, they'll allow you to truly connect with them. It might be the only authentic moment they've had all day. Occasionally, they'll even thank you for making them laugh, since it gave them a chance to take a break from their problems.

People need to laugh, they like to laugh, and they respond to those who give them the permission to laugh. Carl is a better salesman, Joe is a better teacher, Angelo is a better boss, and Roz is a better friend because they each find the humor hidden in life's challenges and are able to communicate this view to others around them. Does that mean you have to be outrageously funny or supremely witty to be a first-class schmoozer? Not at all. But it's important that you see the value of a sunny disposition. All that's required is your willingness to be open to the possibility of playfulness and humor in daily interactions. As my father used to say, "When reaching for the brass ring, don't forget to enjoy the merry-go-round ride."

Think of the people whose smile you most dearly love—your lover, your children, your parents, yourself. If a picture is worth a thousand words, then a smile is worth thousands more! A smile is a picture of one's inner life—one's emotional world. You may wear your heart on your sleeve, but you wear your character on your face. How often in a day do you catch yourself frowning? Do you ever take time to think about what others may be seeing when they look at you? There's nothing more unpleasant and unappealing than a face-to-face interaction with someone whose face is set in a permanent frown. The natural reaction when seeing a sourpuss is to avoid them, mock them, lecture them, or give them a taste of their own medicine. But none of these reactions will help them to lighten up. Perhaps Dorothy isn't aware of how unhappy she appears. Perhaps Gordy refuses to unclench his jaw and other parts of his anatomy. But that shouldn't prevent you from giving them your winning grin. After all, that's what schmoozers do.

Schmoozing requires a lighthearted, playful touch, and a true schmoozer believes in being sincere and sunny, not slippery or fake and phony. Be aware that you can never really fake a smile. No matter how hard you try, your emotional dishonesty will shine through your eyes. It's better to be neutral and natural than funny and fraudulent. You can either endear or estrange yourself from others using humor, so go slowly as you embark upon getting more smileage from your daily encounters. In fact, being funny and allowing others to be funny are two different skills.

To be funny, you need a basic level of understanding about humor, comic timing, verbal acuity, and playful spontaneity. To allow others to be funny, you need to be receptive to their style of humor, especially if it's different from yours. You have to know how to listen, how to sense another person's timing, how to respond to verbal cues, and how to give permission for playful behavior to happen. Don't try too hard to be funny. If you allow others to take the lead and stay alert to how they play, you'll find that your ability to play and be funny will naturally increase.

A witty or clever comment, when tasteful and timely, can put almost anyone in a good mood and pave the way for pleasant and productive relationships. For example, I love to walk up to people who are in a position of authority and say, "Any messages?" If they say, "No, I don't think so...were you expecting some?" I'll respond, "Oh, it's OK, I never get any anyway. I have a very lonely life." By then, they usually sense that I'm not serious, smile, and begin to play along by saying something like,

"Now that I think of it, the Queen did call, but she hung up before I could get her phone number." By the end of the interaction, we're both smiling, and because we have had a chance to share a lighthearted moment, I know we've made a connection. Anytime you can connect or initiate a playful moment with someone, consider yourself fortunate.

I have one method, literally "up my sleeve," for potentially awkward situations that I sense might benefit from a little levity. Before I leave the house, I tuck a small spool of black thread in my shirt pocket and pull the loose end of the thread so that it is the full length of my arm. I then put on my suit coat and pull the thread so that it is hanging out about twelve or thirteen inches from the inside of my jacket sleeve. When I arrive at the event, I introduce myself to someone new. Soon, I'll notice the loose thread dangling from my sleeve, and while still conversing (and with a deadpan look), I'll begin to pull it. Most prudent people will suggest that I cut or break the thread, but I just keep on pulling, and before you know it, I have my hands full of black thread. The person I've just met isn't sure whether to laugh or be concerned that at any moment my sleeve might fall off. If you had nothing to talk about before, you certainly will now.

The objective of this kind of thinking is not to be the center of attention or perform a gag-a-minute, but to find creative and playful ways to break the ice. So throw away your rubber chickens, fake doggie-doo, and whoopee cushions. Less is often more, if not safer. The smart schmoozer's rule (take this as a *gag order*): When in doubt, throw it out! If, however, you desperately want to try a sight gag, make sure to practice it with friends and family before you try it with members of the Common Council.

A Laugh a Day Is the Schmoozers Way

For people with whom you have an ongoing relationship, especially a working relationship, it's always fun to have a "joke of the day" or a "joke of the week." The first thing that many clients, co-workers, and people I know well say to me is; "What's today's joke?" or "What's this week's joke?" They look forward to hearing from me because they know that I will always have a joke ready for them. Many often rely on me to brighten what may be a very stressful day. I make it a point to discover who likes jokes or cartoons, and I'll leave a joke of the week on their voice mail or send them cartoons along with my business correspondence. More often than not, I'll receive something just as funny from them. If you can, keep the jokes G-rated. It doesn't take much talent to use a four-letter word in a joke. And with the growing awareness of the nature of sexual harassment, being crass in the work environment should be a road less and less traveled. You'll find an ample supply of zany cartoons and clean jokes located in the calendar or humor section of your local bookstore. Postcards are also a good source of intelligent humor. I keep a running log of any good jokes I hear by jotting them down on my daily calendar.

A joke log will come in handy if you ever need to address a group and are at a loss for how to open or close your speech. You are a more effective speaker if you know how to use humor to drive home a point. If you are nervous, getting a laugh from an audience can help everyone, especially you, relax. My friend and probably one of the brightest men I have ever met, Dr. Raymond Moody, author of the bestselling books, *Life After Life* and *Laugh After Laugh* (if you are having a problem being humor-impaired, or know someone who is, I strongly recommend these book to help you get over it. They're published by Headwater Press), disarms his audience by beginning his presentations saying, "I have to tell you, I have to tell you, that I have this problem, that I have this problem, where I repeat everything I say, where I repeat everything I say, twice, twice. You will probably get used to this, you will probably get used to this, so please bear with me, so please bear with me." By this time the audience is laughing and praying that he is just kidding. He's got 'em.

Dr. Bernie Siegel sometimes opens his speeches with, "I have some good news and some bad news. The good news is...you're alive. The bad news is…it won't last." If you have a favorite joke or story that works in this type of situation, there's nothing wrong with reusing it, perfecting your delivery, and having it in your back pocket for those rare occasions when you are asked to stand up and speak.

Often what the majority finds funny is what society considers taboo. Those types of jokes are rarely eradicated; they become the domain of comedians in a comedy setting or they simply go underground. If you decide to tell an off-color joke, make sure you know your audience. You can gauge them by the type of jokes they tell. Here's an easy rule to follow: if you're telling an R-rated joke to one person, you can often get away with it. If you are telling two people an off-color joke, one of them—if not both—will judge you. But, if you have enough time-tested jokes, you'll never be the odd man or woman out.

You can increase your ability to use humor by looking for it, appreciating it in others, and being open to trying it yourself. Here are some things that will help sharpen your sense of humor:

- Visit comedy clubs occasionally.

- Imitate your favorite funny lines from television shows or movies.

- Coin a clever phrase, and use it in a variety of settings.

- Hang around people you think are funny, who make you laugh or allow you to be funny.

- Take an improvisation workshop.

- Buy joke books or books of anecdotes for speakers (the best one I can recommend is *The Friar's Club Encyclopedia of Jokes* by H. Aaron Cohl, with an introduction by Allen King, from Black, Dog & Leventhal).

- Rent comedy videos (both movies and stand-up).

- Find a running gag.

- Check out the video list in the Schmick chapter.

- Visit your relatives.

Do whatever brings you more joy, since your joy is bound to rub off on the throngs who will be looking for you to make their day.

So how do you know if you've learned the schmoozer's art of winning by grinning? Next time you are at the Motor Vehicle Department, try to get the people who work there to smile. Add twenty-five thousand points if an inspector laughs and says, "Thanks! You've just made my day." This may sound unbelievable, but a midwestern branch of the Motor Vehicle Department recently became renewal-friendly after learning that a national comedian was ridiculing them by using the backhanded insult, "He had the warm personality of someone who worked at a Motor Vehicle Department." So, if your town has changed the negative reputation of your Motor Vehicle Department, the next best place to test your skills as a schmoozer is with your property assessor. Good luck. Oh, and send me a letter if you're successful.

Finally, here is my list of intravenous video recommendations for getting a grip on life's lighter side. My recommended dosage is at least one a week until you get through this list. If it doesn't work, I'll be interested to know who did your embalming:

- *Harvey*, starring James Stewart

- *Little Shop of Horrors*

- *Being There*, starring Peter Sellers

- *The Princess Bride*, starring Mandy Patinkin

- *Fletch*, starring Chevy Chase

- *Dr. Strangelove*, starring Peter Sellers

- *Network*, starring William Holden

- *Beaches*, starring Bette Midler

- *Heaven Can Wait*, starring Warren Beatty

- *Charlie*, starring Cliff Robinson

- *How to Succeed in Business*, starring Robert Morse

- *Oh God!*, starring George Burns

- *Rain Man*, starring Dustin Hoffman

- *Scrooge*, starring Albert Finney

- Anything by Mel Brooks, but especially *Twelve Chairs*

- *Bill*, starring Mickey Rooney

- *Forrest Gump*, starring Tom Hanks

- *When Harry Met Sally*, starring Billy Crystal and Meg Ryan

- *Dead Poets' Society*, starring Robin Williams

- *Scent of a Woman*, starring Al Pacino

- *Defending Your Life*, starring Albert Brooks

- *Moon over Parador*, starring Richard Dreyfus

- *Harold and Maude*

- *Mary Poppins* (if just for the Ed Wynn laughing scene)

- *Mr. Smith Goes to Washington* (forced watching for the kids)

- *Sling Blade*, starring Billy Bob Thornton

- *The Full Monty*

- and if you haven't watched It's a Wonderful Life by now, you're only asking for the It's a Wonderful Life police to come force you to watch it.

About the Author

Aye Jaye is a performer, stand-up comedian and member of the Clown Hall of Fame. As a performer for an international kids entertainment and advertising corporation, he has entertained millions at Macy's Thanksgiving Day Parade, the Rose Bowl, Radio City Music Hall, hundreds of charitable telethons and has played the White House seven times. He lives with his family near Milwaukee, Wisconsin.

Send us your schmoozes!

If you have performed or received the schmooze of a lifetime—a real full-court schmooze—send it to us! We'd love to hear about it for our next book! Send your ideas to: The Golden Rule of Schmoozing, c/o Sourcebooks, P.O. Box 372, Naperville, IL 60566.